MW00873047

The Fun Dude's Guide to Cruising:
A Humorous Handbook for
Taking Your First Cruise and Living to
Complain About It

By
Jeff "The Fun Dude" Shaw

ISBN-13: 978-1533051417

Cover Photo by Jeremy Yam

Dedication:

To Željka: Your love and companionship make ship life tolerable.
(And—when you're not mad at me—*fun.*)

The Mother of All Disclaimers:

This book is intended as a humorous, tongue-in-cheek exercise in the age-old art of blowing off steam, written, in lieu of expensive psychotherapy, by a stressed-out stand-up comedian who is happily employed by one of the cruise industry's most popular and most customer-friendly cruise lines. The mockery, satire, sarcasm, ridicule, wit, parody and invective contained within are meant to entertain veteran cruisers and crew members alike while making light of the inevitable negative surprises and disappointments awaiting first-time cruisers so that they can be better prepared, avoid having unreasonably high expectations, take any stupid crap that happens with a grain of salt (or perhaps a *whole lotta* salt, around the rim of a margarita glass), and experience so much fun, pleasure and enjoyment on their first cruise that they'll become lifelong cruising aficionados who'll get the logos of their favorite cruise lines tattooed on their foreheads and name their babies after their favorite ships.

Moreover, this admittedly and unabashedly politically incorrect humor book is neither sanctioned nor endorsed by Carnival Cruise Lines or its parent company, Carnival Corporation. Nor does it aim to show the company (or its competitors) in a negative light or scare away potential customers into the arms of Greyhound or Amtrak. In fact, if this book has a target audience, it would have to be the loyal Carnival cruisers who have proven to be some of the best comedy club crowds in the world, who possess above-average senses of humor, and who will all be gloriously chauffeured from this earthly realm aboard a heavenly beam of light once the Rapture comes to pass. (Book now because space is limited!)

And although one could accuse the author of biting the hand that feeds, this is a *humor* book and his opinions have been greatly *exaggerated* for *comedic* effect. Sure, being a huge fan of cruising himself, the author could have written *10* books on the *positive* aspects of cruising, but they'd probably be as *funny* as a fart at a funeral.

OK, so now that the author has covered his *aft*, let's get on with the freaking book, shall we?

Table of Contents

Part 1: Planning Your Cruise

Introduction: "Bon Voyage, Beotch!"

For those of you about to cruise, I salute you. I wish you all a safe, exciting and fun-filled voyage.

Of course, I realize this can't happen for all of you. Some of you will win a huge Bingo jackpot and get run over by an angry granny on a Rascal scooter. Some of you will suffer brain damage in Jet Ski accidents and become fact checkers for Fox News. Some of you will mistake a shark for a dolphin and lose an arm, which will, tragically, cause you to cut your on-board alcohol consumption in half.

Those of you lucky enough to avoid such misfortunes can look forward to lost luggage; noisy neighbors; crying babies; slow Wi-Fi; pushy cab drivers; outrageous ATM fees; tropical storms; hurricanes; tidal waves; diarrhea; gun-toting pirates; manatee attacks; pick-pocketing monkeys; flesh-eating viruses; piranhas in your Speedo; and shape-shifting alien octopuses that will attach themselves to your face, suck out your brains, steal your identity and then charge $10,000 worth of rum cakes to your shipboard account.

Therefore, many of you will not get to enjoy the safe, exciting and fun-filled cruise I'm wishing for you. So just try to have as much fun as you can.

Anyway, ever wonder why your Facebook friends can't stop blabbering about how much fun they had on their latest cruise? They want to make you feel bad, that's why. They know you haven't cruised before so they keep flooding your news feed with posts and photos constantly reminding you about how much they enjoyed themselves in order to make you feel that much sadder about your own miserable, land-locked existence.

But why get sad when you can get even? Now it's your turn to book a cruise, have some fun, and then spend the next six months blogging about and posting photos from your cruise until your friends and relatives kidnap you and take you camping deep in the woods so a team of cult experts can deprogram you.

However, if revenge isn't incentive enough for you to set sail on your dream vacation, then here are a few "fun facts" that just might convince you that your first cruise could very well turn out to be that perfect getaway you've always dreamt about. If not, at least I'll have helped you waste a few minutes of your time you could have spent getting some work done.

Fun Fact #1: Cruises Are Cheap

Cruises offer a big bang for your vacation buck because the fares cover just about everything you'll need for a fun-filled trip: food, accommodations, entertainment and, often, transportation from the airport to the ship. It's a good thing that stuff is included because you're going to need your cash to purchase a $50 tube of sunscreen in Grand Cayman.

You'll often see Internet deals from leading cruise lines for under $100 per person, per night, which is considerably cheaper than you'd spend on land for dinner, drinks and bail.

On some cruise lines, kids even sail for free or at discounted rates when sharing a cabin with two adults. All you have to do is find two adults who won't mind sharing their cabin with your kids.

Fun Fact #2: Cruises Take You to Exotic Locations

Because the ship takes you from one exotic location to another, you won't need to worry about anything but having fun and not getting left behind in Mexico with no luggage, no passport and no Pepto-Bismol.

You'll unpack your suitcase at the beginning of the cruise and wake up in a different tropical paradise every day. Then you'll have to wake up the kids, wait for your friends or relatives to get ready, go to breakfast, realize you're all at different restaurants at different ends of the ship, spend the next half an hour trying to find each other, eat standing up because you're not the only family with the bright idea to eat before disembarking, and then wait in line to get off the ship.

Then, once off the ship, you'll wait for somebody in your party to go back onto the ship for his or her camera, sunglasses or fanny pack. Then you'll stand around in the blazing heat, trying to figure out what to do before realizing that none of you has a clue as to where to go or what to see. So then you'll waste another half an hour irritably negotiating a game plan. Some of you may want to go shopping, some of you may want to go on an excursion, some of you may want to go drinking, and some of you may want to rent a donkey and start the long land trek home. But, in the end, you'll wind up doing what Grandma and Grandpa want to do, which is to visit a Guatemalan sex dungeon.

Fun Fact #3: Cruises Are Family-Friendly

If you're pulling your hair out to find a vacation that your 5-, 10- and 15-year-olds will all love, then go to your local video arcade. But if you want to do something special that will make you and your spouse feel like model parents but that your kids are way too immature and spoiled to enjoy, take the family on a cruise.

Most ships have kids' clubs that are divided by age. Teens have their own cool clubhouse, far away from the playrooms for the rug rats—and even farther away (thank God!) from the adults-only areas. How can your kids not love a kids' club that offers video games, water slide races, dance parties, face painting, arts & crafts and sporting events? Easy, because kids' clubs are "boring," "stupid," and "nowhere near as fun as spending the whole cruise riding up and down the lobby atrium in a glass elevator—awesome!"

So what are you waiting for? Book that first cruise and start making your Facebook friends miserable.

Chapter 1: Why Cruising?

Cruising Is Popular

Cruising is very popular these days. Millions of Americans are trading the campground for the harbor, where they'll board floating cities upon which they can eat their weight in pancakes before lounging around the pool in bikinis and Speedos, forcing their fellow passengers to guzzle large quantities of alcohol in order to blur their vision. This self-perpetuating source of bar revenue enables the leading cruise lines to offer great deals on exciting cruise vacations to glamorous locations, which in turn enables budget-minded vacationers to say goodbye to Cleveland, Ohio, for example, and say hello to Montego Bay, Jamaica, which, coincidentally, is the Cleveland of the Caribbean. (I'm kidding, of course. Cleveland and Montego Bay couldn't be more different: one is a once-glorious city blighted by crumbling infrastructure, litter and crime—and the other is in Ohio.)

Cruising Is Easy

Planning a vacation can be stressful. Trips are fun; planning for one is not. In fact, most people would rather go to the dentist than plan for a trip. (But only if somebody else makes the appointment.)

But whether you book it yourself or go through a travel agent, a cruise is easy to plan for because it's all-inclusive, which means you pay just one low price for food, lodging and entertainment. Unless you want to eat a steak you can chew, in which case you'll have to dine in the upscale steak house—and that costs extra. And unless you want to relax and have fun without your friends or family slowing you down, embarrassing you or driving you crazy, in which case you'll have to book a single-occupancy cabin, and that—you guessed it—costs extra. And unless you want to escape the painful yowling of your inebriated fellow cruisers as they murder Journey's "Don't Stop Believing" for the third time in a row, in which case you'll have to book a karaoke-free cruise—and, cousin, you ain't got that kind of cash.

This one-stop-shopping angle is why cruising has become such an increasingly popular vacation option for lazy landlubbers who would rather save their energy for telling the ship's overworked team members how to do their jobs. (More about the joys of harassing the crew a little later.)

Cruising Is Fun

Another reason you should choose to cruise is cruising is fun. Where else can you eat, read, workout and make love in one place without having to plan your day ahead of time? Prison comes to mind. But wearing a Hawaiian shirt and a fanny pack in prison will get you either shanked or engaged. On a Carnival cruise, however, that's considered formal wear.

My point is that, once you get on the ship, each morning you'll simply read the ship's daily schedule, program or newsletter and underline some fun activities you might like to do that day, such as trivia, Bingo or getting drunk and shouting "woo!" over and over again for no good reason.

Or you can go to the gym for free. You'll find that most of the cardio machines in a cruise ship gym feature video screens so you can watch TV while burning calories. Some of the more upscale luxury liners even feature treadmills with ice cream cone and daiquiri holders so you can *consume* calories while burning calories. (Finally, a good reason for shouting "woo!" over and over again.)

If you have back or knee problems, you can rent a mobility scooter and tool around the ship as drunk as a skunk without worrying about a DUI. But what if you accidentally steer your scooter into the Lido Deck swimming pool? Don't worry. Cruise ship swimming pools are filled with salt water, so your drunk ass will float. As for your scooter, that'll be easy to rescue. Just shout,

"Help—there was a full bucket of beer on that scooter!" and 30 college kids will dive in after it.

Chapter 2: Choosing Your Cruise

Which Line?

The leading cruise lines in North America are Royal Caribbean, Norwegian, Disney, Celebrity, Carnival, Princess and Holland America. Those last three are owned by Carnival Corporation, which is based in Miami, operates over 100 cruise ships and whose newest ship, the Carnival *Vista,* debuted in the spring of 2016. The *Vista* is the first Carnival Fun Ship® to feature an I-Max® theater and pedal-powered sky cars that circle the vessel high above the Lido Deck. She is also the first ship in the Carnival fleet to transform into a giant robot and sink Royal Caribbean ships by first eating her weight in free pizza and ice cream and then attempting to scale Royal Caribbean's la-tee-da rock-climbing walls with a belly full of Fun Farts®.

Although each cruise line offers a variety of cruises at different price points depending on the size of the vessel and her sailing itinerary, each cruise line is known for different things:

1. **Royal Caribbean:** Known for having three of the largest luxury liners sailing out of North America: the *Oasis of the Seas,* the *Allure of the Seas,* and the *John Goodman of the Seas.*
2. **Norwegian:** Known for offering cruises to just about every country in the world except Norway.
3. **Disney:** Known for not having casinos. (Donald Duck doesn't wear pants yet they want to protect your family from *gambling*?)
4. **Celebrity:** Ironically, known for hiring "big-name" entertainers no one's ever heard of.
5. **Carnival:** Known as a haven for hacky humor book writers.
6. **Princess:** Known for making opulence affordable for people who can neither spell nor define "opulence."

7. **Holland America:** Known for dirt cheap rentals of walkers, scooters and oxygen tanks.

Which Ship?

After selecting your cruise line, you'll need to pick your ship. Most of the leading lines have several ships to choose from. To narrow down your search you'll need to decide how much money you want to spend, where you want to sail to and how long you want to be at sea. You can then comb each cruise line's website to see which ships fit those criteria. You may also want to consider whether you want a big ship or small ship; old ship or new. Every fleet has its newer, ritzier ships that boast branded spaces and popular amenities such as yoga classes; Tai-Chi; miniature golf; obstacle courses; water slides; 3-D theaters; zip lines; rock climbing walls; wave pools; ice skating rinks; bull fighting arenas; demolition derbies; Renaissance fairs; wild boar hunting; elephant rides; NASA rocket launches (seasonal); and alpaca farms, where you can shear and sew your own souvenir sweater. Royal Caribbean has the *Ovation of the Seas,* Norwegian has the *Escape,* Disney has the *Fantasy,* Celebrity has the *Reflection,* Carnival has the *Vista,* Princess has the *JAP,* and Holland America has the *Wheezing Geezer.*

These ships tend to be more elegant and exciting but also tend to be more expensive and more crowded. Royal Caribbean's *Ovation of the Seas,* for example, holds 100,000 passengers, employs 50 crew members and boasts one public restroom (one stall for gents; one stall for ladies). A typical fare for a seven-day sailing on a vessel this magnificent costs around $50,000 for an inside cabin and $1 million for an ocean-view cabin. (They might have a few cabins near the ice machines that you can snag for $40 a night, but only if you're a heavy sleeper and don't expect there to be any ice in the machine the one time you decide to pop outside your cabin to use it.)

The leading cruise lines also have older, smaller ships which offer much cheaper fares than the newer additions to their fleets. Although these ships can look a little rough around the edges, they're usually kept impeccably clean and meticulously maintained, thanks to an army of midget Filipinos living under the stairs. And although you may feel as if you're traveling on a floating motel instead of on a glamorous ocean liner, these ships offer short-but-sweet cruises at ridiculously low prices while exuding a very pleasant, upbeat and personal vibe. These ships, such as Carnival's Fun Ship *Ramada,* Norwegian's SS *Minnow* (featuring a new *four-hour* tour, May thru September only) and Royal Caribbean's *Winnebago of the Seas,* cater mostly to either first-time cruisers wanting to see if cruising appeals to them or to frequent cruisers who live near the port and enjoy drinking themselves silly without slamming their car into a tree.

How Long?

With luxury cruise lines, the smaller the ship, the more elegant and exclusive it is. With mainstream lines, the smaller the ship, the dingier and more run-down it is; therefore, these ships tend to attract loads of party people who have real no interest in exploring Nassau or Freeport for the umpteenth time but simply want to swill as much firewater as humanly possible in three days without having to shell out perfectly good drinking money on an Uber. These voyages are affectionately referred to in the industry as "booze cruises," and the cruisers as "boozers." Booze cruises can be very economical. For example, a three-day booze cruise aboard the Carnival *Libation* costs 50 cents per day, per person, per cabin. On the other hand, you'll still be paying off your bar tab long after you've paid off your mortgage. Fortunately, Carnival will sometimes accept your children as payment. (Don't worry: drink enough and you'll make more.)

If a 3- or 4-day cruise to the Bahamas sounds too long for you, a few cruise lines offer special 2-day "Cruises to Nowhere," which go to Detroit.

But if you're in the mood for a longer, more substantial cruising experience, the most common cruise itineraries last seven days, leaving homeport on a Saturday or Sunday and returning a week later (for those of you having trouble with the concept of "seven days"). However, many cruise lines offer special cruises lasting 14 days, 30 days or more. These are usually special one-off cruises to South America, Alaska, Hawaii or any other exotic destination that is too expensive and time-consuming to sail to from Florida, Baltimore, Long Beach or New York. These special itineraries offer regular cruisers a change of scenery and the crew more time to get to know their passengers so they can hate them for more reasons than simply because they're Americans. Moreover, all cruise lines offer special repositioning cruises, such as when a brand-new Carnival ship finishes its inaugural season of European runs and then returns to its permanent homeport in the States for the sole purpose of getting the staff and crew super excited about finally trading boring Venice, Italy, for, say, super-exciting Port Canaveral, Florida, complete with shuttle bus service to Wal-Mart.

To decide how long of a cruise is best for you, you'll need to consider your budget, how much time you or your family members can get off from work or school, and how long your family can spend cooped up together without killing each other.

Not sure you can go on a family cruise vacation without the Coast Guard getting involved? Then, before deciding how long of a cruise you want to book, you might first want to consider….

Chapter 3: Who's Going?

Cruising by Yourself

Feel like going on a cruise but are afraid your friends or family members will spoil your fun with their constant bitching and moaning?

Then screw 'em—cruise by yourself. You don't need friends and family making you miserable on your cruise when you're perfectly capable of making yourself miserable.

Cruising alone definitely has its benefits. Some ships, such as the Norwegian *Wood,* feature special cabins, nightclubs and dining areas for solo cruisers. Of course, going solo also has its drawbacks. First of all, you can go blind. Secondly, most cruise lines will pad your fare with something known as the "single supplement," which is an extra charge that penalizes you for being too smart to cruise with your friends and family even though it's not hard for a genius like you to realize that your friends and family are the main reason you need a vacation to begin with. This add-on can range anywhere from 10 percent of the cruise fare to the same price as two passengers in one cabin. But if you figure in how much less vodka you'll be drinking and how much less Xanax you'll be popping if you leave your loved ones behind, the single supplement can seem more like a "sanity surcharge."

Moreover, cruising alone can be lots of fun because you'll get to do things you normally wouldn't get to do when burdened by traveling companions. You'll get to:

- Explain over and over again to complete strangers why you're cruising alone.
- Attend a "singles' mingle," where you can lose yourself in an intimate conversation with your bartender because you'll be the only two people there.

- Get extra dessert from your dining-room waiters because seeing how pitiful you look dining alone reminds them of how much they miss their loved ones back home.
- Walk around in your underwear because you won't have a cabin mate around to constantly nag you to go back to the cabin and put on some pants.
- Spend less time arguing about what to do and where to meet and spend more time looking for a sugar mama or a sugar daddy.

In many ways, cruising is a perfect vacation choice for solo travelers. Some cruise lines treat single cruisers to soirees that allow them to socialize with other single cruisers. They figure that the faster you start spending the night in somebody else's cabin, the faster they can put somebody else in yours and start charging you double.

Some cruise lines, mostly those that cater to older guests, such as Cocoon Cruise Lines International, even hire "gentlemen dance hosts" so that classy-yet-absentminded widows traveling alone will have someone to accuse of stealing the jewelry they actually forgot at home.

Cruising with Friends

Sometimes, cruising with a big group of friends or coworkers can be by far the best way to cruise. What's more fun than spending thousands of dollars to embark upon the vacation of a lifetime only to spend three quarters of every day waiting for everybody to make up their minds about what to do and where to meet?

You'll find that the tacit obligation to spend every waking moment together will create a special bond between you and your travel mates that can only be broken when you push one of them overboard and start dancing around in unbridled glee like Cam Newton after a touchdown.

Just like with anything else in life, advanced planning is the key to a successful group cruise. So here are three useful tips for planning a group cruise:

1. **Pick a group leader.** This person will do the majority of the grunt work involved in researching, planning and booking the cruise. This person should always be the least popular person in the group. That way, he won't feel guilty for coming and you won't feel guilty for not wanting him there.
2. **Choose your cruise diplomatically.** It's not easy finding the perfect cruise for a group of 10 to 50 people of varying ages, interests and gastrointestinal disorders. The first task of the group leader is to figure out how to choose the best cruise so that everyone will be happy. Once the group leader realizes that this will never ever happen, his next task is to eat an entire carton of mint chocolate chip ice cream in the middle of the night with the lights off while hatching a plan to fake his own death.
3. **Book early.** Early bookings are essential for anyone who...

- Wants to travel during the summer or school holidays.
- Wants the best cabins on the newest ships, for a specific voyage.
- Wants as many members of the group as possible to cancel at the last minute.

Cruising with Family

Close to three million children under the age of 18 went on cruises last year. There are two reasons for this:

1. To entice and entertain junior cruisers, most cruise lines offer meet and greets with famous cartoon characters; video game tournaments; water slides; zip lines; obstacle courses; dance parties; and a relatively new and increasingly popular competition wherein children kill each other with bows and arrows until the last brat standing gets to take leftover ship food back home to her starving village.
2. Their grandparents didn't think they could handle watching them for an entire week.

All of the major cruise lines offer teen-friendly cruises that cater to families with hard-to-please adolescents. You'll just need to compare each line's teen programs to determine which ship offers the best variety of fun and interesting activities your kids will choose to ignore so they can spend the entire cruise riding up and down the glass elevators in the ship's lobby instead. (Yes, this joke has already appeared earlier in the book but, hey, if you can't handle hearing the same lame joke over and over again, you can't handle a week on a cruise ship.)

The great thing about cruising is that even tiny tots can get in on the fun. Most cruise lines have special programs designed to excite the imagination of the little sea urchins in your family:

1. **Disney:** Your kindergartener can enjoy a tea party with Cinderella while his older sister does battle with a Marvel Superhero (or vice versa).
2. *Norwegian*: Your kids can dance with "Dora the Explorer," sing along with "SpongeBob Square Pants" or smoke a blunt with "Jay and Silent Bob." Wait a second—I'm talking about little kids here, so perhaps that joke isn't appropriate. Let's change it to *or eat pot brownies with "Jay and Silent Bob."*
3. **Carnival:** Toddlers love Carnival's new "Seuss at Sea" program, including the "Seuss-a-palooza Parade and Story Time," as well as the "Green Eggs and Ham Breakfast." Yes, little ones *love* these events. So don't let the incessant screeching and crying of every rug rat in attendance fool you.
4. **Royal Caribbean**: Your kids will be put to work shoveling coal in the engine room.

Chapter 4: Booking Your Cruise

Regardless of how much money you have in the bank or how big your vacation budget is, getting the lowest possible fare on a cruise is always a plus. That way, you'll have some money left over for plastic surgery so that you can shake those IRS investigators off your tail before boarding a luxury ocean liner bound for the Cayman Islands. Unfortunately, finding good deals can be tough sometimes because a luxury cruise to a popular destination can be a little pricey. So here are six tips to help you prevent your next cruise vacation from costing you an arm and a nose job:

1. **Book through a travel agent.** If you're worried that going through a third party will make your cruise more expensive, stop worrying. Travel agents make their money on commissions from cruise lines, wholesalers and hotels—and from all the marijuana they sell on the side, which is nothing compared to the amount they smoke. Yes, it shouldn't surprise you that *all* travel agents are high *all* the time. That's why they're always telling you not to worry: "But what if one of my relatives has to cancel the cruise for any reason, such as being arrested for flying his gyrocopter into White House airspace—will I get the deposit for his fare back?" *Don't worry, dude. Just mellow out and everything's gonna be OK, dude.* "One half of my party has the six o'clock dinner seating, one half has the eight o'clock dinner seating, and the third half is brown-bagging it. Are you sure the Maître D' will be able to change our dining times around so we can all eat together?" *All this talk of dinner is making me hungry, dude. Stay on the line while I skateboard down to Sam's Club and snag a 10-pound bag of M & M's, dude.* Because travel agents always have access to righteous weed, they're able to trade for special cruise deals not available to the general public, and therefore they can end up saving you big bucks on your cruise. And the great this is their assistance won't cost you a dime—or even a dime *bag.* Just

bring them back a suitcase full of rum cake from the Bahamas and they'll call it even, *dude.*

2. **Book at the last minute.** If your travel plans are flexible, you should seriously consider holding off until the last minute to book your cruise. The closer they get to the departure date, the more desperate cruise lines become to offload unsold cabins at bargain-basement rates meant to lure you into quitting your job and selling your children (try Craig's List!) so you can just pick up and go. Since the ship is going to sail regardless of whether she's completely full or half empty, they figure that they can't sell expensive cocktails and Bingo cards to empty cabins. Play your cards right and you can net huge savings with this strategy. However, keep in mind that some ships with popular itineraries are always going to be jam-packed at certain times of the year, so be sure to read my companion piece to this book, "Hey, Jackass—Don't Wait till the Last Minute to Book Your Cruise!"

3. **Cruise at the right time of the year.** The best time to cruise is definitely during spring break. Especially if you're older, cruising alone to just get away from it all, or simply looking for a romantic getaway with that special coworker of the opposite sex who is married but not to you. The great thing about cruising during spring break is that the ship will be booked to capacity either with grade-schoolers running around screaming, shouting and peeing on everything; or, with college kids running around screaming, shouting and peeing on everything. Either way, all that screaming, shouting and peeing will make your cruise seem all that much more adventurous and exciting. You might even pee a little yourself.

4. **Look into added-value promotions.** Many cruise lines offer special deals that might include hotel rooms, discounted or complimentary shore excursions, and perhaps even included or discounted airfare. Only problem is you'll have to book these cruises a little in advance, say, a decade or two. You may be able to find even more added-value promotions

through a travel agent, such as free Skittles and rolling papers. (If you haven't caught on yet, *all* travel agents are high *all* the time.)

5. **Check out cruise consolidators.** If you choose to bypass a travel agent, consider checking out cruise consolidators or "bulk buyers" who buy blocks of cabins at incredible discounts. Cruise consolidators can snag you considerable savings on cabins, excursions and such. Just keep in mind that all cruise consolidators work for the Mafia, so if you cancel your cruise for any reason, you just might end up as a sightseeing stop for future divers and snorkelers.

6. **Create a budget and stick to it.** Ha! Ha! Ha! I'm killing me.

So there you have it. Six tips for saving *mucho dinero* on your *proximo crucero*. As good as money in the bank. (Or maybe an offshore account in the Caymans.)

Booking through a Travel Agent

Booking a cruise can be a bit overwhelming. But, before you do anything, you have to decide how much you're willing to pay and whether to make do with a cheap inside cabin ("What do I need a balcony for?") or spoil yourself with a balcony ("Then again, I might feel like pushing my spouse overboard."), and which cruise line and ship are right for your budget. Throw travel mates, dinner seating times, shore excursions and cabin locations into the mix, and planning a relaxing vacation can become more complicated than planning a bank heist.

You might assume that the only way to book a cruise in the computer age is online. But, because booking online can often be confusing, you might want to hire a travel agent. A travel agent—especially one who is high all the time—has much more experience with being confused than you do and can therefore confuse you much better than you can confuse yourself.

One of the most important things to know is that travel agents who specialize in cruises have been on lots of ships and can therefore give you expert advice about different cruise options. They take familiarization trips and go to cruise line seminars so you don't have to do the research yourself. (Actually, they take those trips to get lucky and go to those seminars to get stoned, but they're still saving you the research.)

Better yet, travel agents often have access to special discounts or perks that you'll never find on your own and that never ever seem to apply to your particular cruise. And because the cruise lines pay their commissions, you don't have to pay for their help. Just be prepared to leave voicemail after desperate voicemail when you realize that, not only did your reefer-rolling travel agent forget to tell you that you wouldn't get your deposit back if you needed to cancel your cruise (nor did he broach the subject of travel insurance), but you've also discovered that he entered your personal information into the computer incorrectly and now the cruise line has no record of your booking.

Booking It Yourself

Of course, going through a travel agent isn't always necessary. Here's how to determine if it's OK to book on your own:

1. **You have experience.** If you've cruised before and know exactly what you want, then you're a mutant who needs to be preserved in a laboratory for scientific study. So, OK, let's say you *are* a mutant who knows exactly what you want—which cruise line, which ship, which itinerary, which type of cabin, and which members of your family you want to stay home—booking your cruise online can be as easy as 1-2-2-2-2-2-2-2-2 (don't you hate it when your laptop keys stick?). Most cruise booking websites (more about booking online later) feature thorough search capability along with pages that list their latest and greatest deals and steals. Many also offer bonus tools, such as deck plans, photos and reviews. Step-by-step instructions will guide you through the booking and

payment procedures. Fortunately, you'll find that almost all of these sites are programmed to freeze the moment you click on "Confirm Booking," forcing you to repeat all of the steps over and over again until you become a certified cruise booking expert.

2. **You're a DIY type.** If you have the time and inclination to thoroughly research your own trip using resources like *Cruise Critic,* then go right ahead. Then, if you make mistakes that result in a few unpleasant surprises once you board your ship, you can become bitter and depressed, which, by the way, is the perfect mood for writing a review of your cruise on *Cruise Critic.*

Booking Online

Booking cruises online is becoming increasingly popular thanks to the fact that most sites are very user-friendly now and because people are in general becoming more and more comfortable buying stuff off the Internet. Therefore, more travelers than ever are opting for the convenience of searching for great cruise deals online. Here is my one and only pointer to help you avoid the most common mistake when booking your cruise online without the help of a doobie-toking travel agent:

1. **Make sure you're connected to the Internet.** The most common mistake beginners make when trying to book a cruise online is not realizing that they actually have to be connected to the Internet first. Not to be a smart ass (whom am I trying to kid—*of course* I'm trying to be a smart ass), but that's what being "online" means. It means being connected to the Internet. So if you're not connected to the Internet, then you can't be online. Which means you can't book a cruise online. So don't waste time running a Google search for "cheap cruises," because you have to be online in order to run a Google search. So if you don't know how to connect your computer to the Internet, maybe you should just enlist

the help of a bong-hitting travel agent after all. They're actually quite easy to find. All you have to do is get totally baked and then run a Google search for "bonng httting traaavul aggunt."

Chapter 5: Preparing for Your Cruise

Researching

Before you go on your cruise, take advantage of all the amazing resources on the Internet to become familiar with your ship and the ports you'll be visiting. Explore your ship's website to check out the deck plan, see where you cabin is located, what entertainment is offered on board and which shore excursions are available. Make sure you look at as many photos as possible of the various public areas because, when you're finally on the ship, your view will be obstructed by a never-ending parade of big-butted cruisers in search of free cookies and ice-cream like some sort of hypoglycemic zombies.

You can check the leading travel websites to learn where to go in port, what to see, what to eat, as well as what to be wary of. For example, if you do your homework on Cozumel, Mexico, one of most frequented ports in the Caribbean, you'll learn that you can't use an ATM without having your identity stolen; can't walk down the street during the daytime without being harangued into buying a horse blanket with an NFL team logo on it; can't walk down the street at night without being robbed; and will find that authentic Mexican food costs way more than the items on the Taco Bell 99-Cent Value Menu back in the States:

HUNGRY TOURIST/FREQUENT TACO BELL CUSTOMER:
(Reading menu)

"Fifteen dollars—for *one* enchilada?!"

AUTHENTIC MEXICAN WAITER IN AUTHENTIC MEXICAN RESTAURANT:

"Si. Would you like chicken or beef?"

HUNGRY TOURIST/FREQUENT TACTO BELL CUSTOMER:

"For *fifteen* dollars there better be *cocaine* in my enchilada!"

AUTHENTIC MEXICAN WAITER IN AUTHENTIC MEXICAN RESTAURANT:

"No problema. But that will cost one dollar extra."

Another thing you really should know is that Mexico's national pastime is driving a taxi cab. Everybody drives a cab in Mexico. Men, women, children—you might even see a donkey behind the wheel. (Of course, being from America, you should be used to taking cabs driven by jackasses.)

Dieting

Most first-time cruisers feel compelled to diet during the months leading up to their vacation so that they'll look good in a bikini, Speedo or, at the very least, their warm-weather clothes such as shorts and tank tops. But if you really want to fit in on your cruise, you're going to want to go the other way and eat as much as possible so that you won't attract unwanted attention once you finally board your ship. If you strut around the Lido Deck in swimwear, revealing sculpted arms, six-pack abs and an air of self-confidence, you're bound to draw the ire of your fellow cruisers. They'll mock you and harass you for having the audacity to show off a healthy body in public—on a cruise ship, of all places. OK, well at least in *theory.* In *reality,* it's doubtful anyone will stop feeding his or her face long enough to look up, let alone actually say anything to you.

After spending countless hours scouring hundreds of nutrition and dieting websites, I've come up with a suggested diet you can follow anywhere from two weeks to three months before you cruise:

Breakfast: Ice cream.

Lunch: Pizza.

Dinner: Pizza and ice cream.

And because every cruise ship has a fully equipped passenger gym, it might be a good idea to join a gym at home at least six months prior to your cruise. That way, you'll already be used to not going to the gym and won't be bothered by feelings of guilt or regret for not using the gym on the ship.

Clothes Shopping

Cruising is a great excuse for splurging on a new wardrobe. In order to *feel* good you need to *look* good, right? Well, then head to the mall, max out those credit cards, and get yourself some stylish new duds for your cruise. Unless you're going on an Alaskan cruise, you'll want to update your warm-weather wardrobe for you and your family. You'll need new loungewear, new swimwear, new beachwear, new formal wear, new casual wear and new sleepwear. You'll also need new casual footwear, new formal footwear, new gym shoes, new slippers, new sandals and new flippers for snorkeling. You'll also need new accessories such as new belts, new ties, new scarves, new watches, new jewelry, new cologne and new sunglasses. And although you'll be dying from anticipation, do *not* wear any of your new stuff at home—save every last stitch of your new wardrobe for your cruise. And make sure to leave all the price tags on everything; because, as soon as you get on the ship, you'll realize you're too tired to unpack and in no mood to iron anything, so you'll wind up wearing the same gym shorts and T-shirt you arrived in for the entire voyage.

Chapter 6: Packing for Your Cruise

What to Bring

One of the big advantages of cruising is that you only have to unpack once. Unless you're a man, in which case you don't even need to pack in the first place. Most guys can make do with the clothes on their back. They start to stink, they jump into the pool. But if you're a woman (if you're not sure, ask someone), don't think you'll have to live out of your suitcase. Every cruise ship cabin has ample storage space for your clothes—sometimes an entire drawer, in addition to a giant one foot by two feet closet with three tiny hangers in it. So go ahead and bring whatever you need to look good and feel good, but remember that, if you're flying, the airlines charge extra for overweight luggage and additional pieces of luggage, and the average amount the typical air traveler pays in luggage fees per flight is somewhere around the price of a cruise.

So try to pack light. And if you forget anything, you can probably buy it in the ship's gift shop or at any of the shops in the ports for only three to four times as expensive.

The three biggest considerations when packing for your cruise are:

1. Are you cruising to a tropical climate (the Caribbean) or an arctic climate (Wisconsin)?
2. Which ship will you be cruising on?
3. Who will be carrying your suitcase?

If the answer to #3 is "Me," then just bring one set of clothes and plan to shower with them on whenever you smell ripe. But if somebody else will be carrying your luggage, then it's time to start packing like Madonna going on tour.

Dress Codes

Dress codes have become considerably more relaxed in recent years ever since the cruise lines realized that slobs have money, too. In the daytime, you can wear whatever you want: tank tops, shorts, jeans, bathing suits (the fatter and hairier you are, the better) — anywhere on the ship. Unless, of course, you opt for a sit-down lunch in one of the main dining rooms, in which case you'll be asked to either put on a shirt or shave your back.

What you should wear at night can vary from ship to ship and where you choose to eat dinner. If you wish to eat in the main dining room, you'll have to adhere to the dress code, which is usually a suit and tie for men and a cocktail dress or pantsuit for ladies on formal night and "dress casual" outfits on the other nights. But if you're going to eat dinner in one of the casual eateries, such as the Lido Deck buffet, just try not to show up naked unless you have a really hot body. (You don't.)

When packing for a cruise, don't forget something nice to wear on formal night. If you don't own a tuxedo or evening gown, a tank top or sweatpants will do just fine. Just make sure they're *clean.* It *is* formal night, after all.

On some cruise lines, formal night isn't what it used to be. Dressing up is now optional on my ship because my cruise line doesn't want to alienate the lucrative "Duck Dynasty" demo by forcing them to wear anything that needs to be ironed. From a business standpoint, that makes perfect sense: Disgruntled guests spend less money so why risk upsetting a high roller who won't even splurge on a pair of $10 dress slacks at T.J. Maxx?

Before making formal night more convenient for the sartorially challenged, the cruise lines need to ask themselves, "What kind of nighttime atmosphere do we want to promote on our ships? An elegant atmosphere where guests can delight in looking their very best for a couple of hours? Or a relaxed atmosphere where guests can enjoy a refined seven-course meal in swimsuits and flip-flops? Do we want guests to feel like they're on a luxurious ocean liner in the Caribbean or at a KOA in Jacksonville?"

Oddly, some cruise lines seem to care more about the wants and needs of their less sophisticated first-time cruisers than those of their more urbane repeat guests. Unfortunately, the more they coddle the common folk, the more they devalue their classier customers who are more appreciative, more cooperative, and tend to spend more money on board. But because classier guests tend to grumble less, many cruise lines have started to tailor their policies to the complaints and grievances of a few flip-flop philistines who, for example, feel discriminated against because "them treadmills in the guest gym ain't got no ashtrays."

Although my cruise line does it's best to make all guests feel equally special, if I tell some shirtless biker with a giant flaming skull tattoo on his chest that he can't enter my comedy club before donning the "Who Farted?" tank top he has slung over his shoulder like a "Captain Trailer Park" cape, he'll wheel his pimped-out Rascal Scooter down to Guest Services and threaten to have his entire Hell's Angels chapter boycott the cruise line. So, of course, my cruise director is forced to give in and tell the guest that, because we truly value the patronage of a part-time drug mule who bought his cruise at the last minute on CheapAssCruises.com thanks to the $200 settlement he got on "Judge Judy," the giant flaming skull tattoo on his chest does indeed count as a shirt.

"But, Boss," I'll say, "What about all the wealthy platinum and diamond members sitting next to him in their tuxedos and evening gowns with looks of disgust and astonishment on their faces?"

"Well, if they're so wealthy, how come they can't afford a nice tank top for formal night?"

What Not to Bring

Don't Bring: A clothes iron. Irons are banned industry wide for two reasons: 1) Fire is one of the biggest dangers on a cruise ship; 2) If you bring an iron, the ship can't charge you seven dollars to press your shirt for you. Besides, a few lines like Carnival and Holland America have self-service launderettes with ironing boards. Royal Caribbean and Norwegian don't. So you're actually going to have to: a) Pay an ungodly sum to have your suit or dress pressed (usually twice the amount you originally paid for it); b) Hang it the bathroom for an hour with the shower on Hot; or c) Go to dinner more wrinkled than Larry King's ass.

Do Bring: Wrinkle-releasing spray. Simply spray onto your wrinkled, crumpled, rumpled, disheveled or creased article of clothing. And then tug, smooth out with your hand, and *voilà:* You now have an article of clothing that is wrinkled, crumpled, rumpled, disheveled or creased and *wet.*

Don't Bring: Swiss Army knife. You're not camping, you idiot—you're cruising! They've got Filipinos to open your beer bottles for you!

Do Bring: Axe shower gel, shampoo and body spray (for men). Although all cruise lines provide soap, shampoo, conditioner and body lotion, a sexy world traveler such as yourself doesn't leave home without his full line of Axe products. Get clean with Axe and you'll get "dirty" on your cruise.

Don't Bring: Heroin. Not a single cruise line allows you to bring smack aboard. That's because they want you to buy your smack from them in their on-board duty-free shops. See? That's how they get you.

Do Bring: Water and soda. Although most lines let you bring on a "reasonable" amount of bottled water and soda, a few of them forbid bottled water due to the fact that many passengers have been caught trying to smuggle alcohol hidden in water bottles.

Now, with the high price of bottled water on board, passengers have been sneaking water on in liquor bottles.

Don't Bring: Books. Books are heavy, take up space and make you look smart, which can make it hard for you to make friends with your fellow cruisers, who'll be walking around barefooted, shouting (as mentioned earlier) "woo!" for no reason whatsoever. Besides, if you want to read books, most ships have libraries with the latest titles (*The Scarlet Letter* and *Ivanhoe*) to sign out—if the crew member assigned to library duty didn't forget to bring the bookcase key with her because she's hung-over from the night before.

Do Bring: An e-reader such as a Nook or Kindle. Packing a Kindle instead of a bunch of hardcovers will not only save you weight and space in your luggage but also help you meet all kinds of interesting people who will ask you, "So, how do you like your Kindle?" To which you can reply, "I'm not sure, because every time I sit down to read it, some nosy dipshit tries to start a conversation with me."

Banned Items

If you don't want to have anything confiscated by Security at check-in, it's a good idea to familiarize yourself with items that are banned pretty much by every cruise line:

1. **Firearms and ammunition:** Sorry, but no guns allowed. Like it or not, ladies, you're just going to have to get your husband to shut up the old fashioned way: by pushing him overboard.
2. **Sharp objects:** Including all knives and scissors with blades over four inches long. Machetes are allowed but only if intended for use on off-key karaoke singers.
3. **Illegal drugs and substances:** If you want to get high on a cruise ship, you're just going to have to cross your fingers and hope you run into a travel agent.

4. **Candles and incense:** These are fire hazards. So, if you want your cabin to smell like vanilla, you're just going to have to spill ice cream on the carpet like everyone else.

5. **Coffee makers, clothes irons, heating pads and hot plates:** Fire hazard! Fire hazard! Fire hazard! Fire hazard!

6. **One Direction CDs:** Fire hazard! (If you're in the cabin next to mine and you leave your door open, I will sneak in and melt your One Direction CDs with your coffee maker, clothes iron, heating pad or hot plate.)

7. **Baseball bats, hockey sticks, bows and arrows, pepper spray, handcuffs, nightsticks, lighter fluid and fireworks:** Hey, Casanova—leave the sex toys at home!

8. **Floatation devices:** Items such as rafts, inner tubes, body boards and water wings cannot be used in the swimming pools on board because the cruise lines would prefer it if your children drowned.

9. **Alcoholic beverages:** No, you can't bring booze aboard! Who do you think you are—the Captain?!

10. **T-shirts or hats with slogans playing off the word "ship":** Although you may think catchphrases such as "Ship happens," "You don't know ship," "Drunk as ship," "Time to get ship faced" or "Same ship, different day" are unique and clever, your ship's crew and staff members have heard it all a million times before. So don't be surprised if they lose control and beat you to death with life-raft oars. But, hey, ship happens.

Part 2: Starting Your Cruise

Chapter 7: Boarding the Ship

The Shuttle Bus

In June of 2015, I treated my parents to a cruise aboard the Carnival *Pride* for their 50th wedding anniversary. The reason we chose the *Pride* is because she's a beautiful and classy ship that sails out of Baltimore, a mere six-hour drive from Cleveland. Not having to purchase three airfares to Port Canaveral, Miami or New Orleans saved me thousands of dollars, which I used instead to park our car in the port's parking garage.

So, unless you can afford to fork out several grand to park for a week, you'll probably be flying to your ship's homeport. Most of the airports near major seaports offer a shuttle bus service. At the Orlando airport, for example, a company called Mears operates a fleet of big, shiny, yellow buses bound for Port Canaveral. The advantage of taking the Mears shuttle to your ship is that most of the folks on the bus will be your shipmates for the next week and so the 45-minute bus ride will give you plenty of time for you to decide whom you'll want to socialize with, whom you'll want to avoid, and whom you'll find so instantly and overwhelming annoying that you'll start fantasizing about the bus going over a cliff and bursting into flames. But then, when you finally arrive at the pier less than an hour later, your aggravation will be replaced first with exhilaration from seeing your ship up close for the first time and then with frustration after realizing that there are no cliffs between Orlando and Port Canaveral.

The Terminal

After exiting the shuttle bus, gathering your luggage and declining to tip the bus driver because, even though you had five dollars for him rolled up in your front pocket the whole time, you changed your mind after listening to him utter, "Gratuities are appreciated!" over the loud speaker every five minutes, it's time to head into the terminal and check-in. Correction: It's time to get in line and wait about an hour to get into the terminal and check in. This is why they're called cruise *lines*. And, while waiting in line, you might see some folks breeze right past you. These people have "priority boarding status," obtained by cruising a certain number of times in the past, by paying a small fee or by being members of the Illuminati.

When checking in, you'll get your boarding pass, run your credit card for incidentals, and then get the best workout of your life by trying to get your suitcase to fit in the pier security luggage scanner. Everyone in your traveling party will have tried to convince you to just have it loaded onto the ship with the other luggage but you just wouldn't listen so now you'll have to open it, unpack it, repack it, reclose it and then sit on it so it'll make it through the scanner without the conveyor belt snapping. This will be the second most embarrassing experience of your cruise. The *most* embarrassing will be trying to fit your fat ass into your cabin's tiny shower.

The Gangway and Ship's Lobby

After checking in and going through the security checkpoint, it's time to head to the gangway. Most cruise ships have you enter through the lobby, which is usually on the third or fourth deck, so you'll have to walk along a glass-encased gangway up to the ship, allowing you to take in the full majesty of the vessel, all the hustle and bustle on the pier, and all the missing nuts and bolts on the glass-encased gangway.

When you finally exit the gangway and enter the lobby of the ship, you'll be struck by one of two feelings: You'll either take in the grandeur of this magnificent floating city and be glad you splurged on a more modern, more elegant ship, or you'll look at the outdated and timeworn décor of your low-priced ship and think that maybe you should've gone Greyhound.

The lobby of the ship is where you can wait in line at Guest Services to complain about how unsatisfied you are about all 15 minutes of your cruising experience so far, wait in line to purchase a shore excursion, wait in line to purchase an alcoholic beverage or soft drink program, and listen to a sleep-deprived DJ spin teeth-rattling gangster rap designed to get you in the mood for a relaxing Caribbean vacation.

The lobby is also a good place to meet various members of the ship's staff and crew. If you want these folks to approach you, adopt a confident stride and pretend like you're familiar with the layout of the ship and know exactly where you're going. The more you look as if you don't need any help, the more likely they'll offer it, because they know you'll say, "No thanks, I'm good." But if you look like you're completely lost, overwhelmed and about to cry, that means they'll really have to put some effort and energy into assisting you and so they'll treat you as if you're a mosquito carrying the Zika virus and take off running and screaming in the other direction.

Ship's Security

The first crew members you'll meet will most likely be your ship's security guards, because they're the ones who'll confiscate the drugs and alcohol you try to sneak on board and properly dispose of them at the next crew party. These dedicated men and woman, usually from India or the Philippines, work around the clock to keep the ship and everyone on her safe. For example, should you find yourself dancing the night away in the ship's disco when a crazy, free-for-all bar fight breaks out just like in the movies, you can rest assured that an entire squad of fully trained and fully equipped members of the ship's crack Security Team will appear in seconds, ready to swiftly and surgically neutralize the situation by making sure that every crew member watching the fight is in the proper uniform and wearing his or her nametag.

Ship's Photographers

The second group of crew members you'll meet will definitely be the ship's photographers. Their job is to make you feel like a glamorous movie star during your cruise by stalking you like a member of the Paparazzi. They'll take your picture everywhere:

- On the gangway
- In the lobby
- By the pool
- In the dining room
- In the nightclub
- In the shower
- On the toilet
- On the rescue boat sent to pull you out of the ocean after you jump overboard in a desperate attempt to escape the ship's photographers

Not only will the ship's photographers try to *take* as many photos of you and your traveling companions as possible, they'll also try to *sell* you as many photos of you and your traveling companions as possible by publicly displaying each and every photo they take so that you can pick and choose the ones you like. All you'll have to do is make your way to the ship's photo gallery every evening and inspect the day's work. If you have trouble finding your photos, ask the ship's photo gallery manager for assistance. He or she will help you locate your most recent shots by using the latest in face recognition technology. Meaning, he or she will look through every single photo in the gallery until finding the ones that match your face.

Then, all you'll have to do is decide which photos you want, how many copies you want, what format you want them in, and which price package works best for you. Then, you'll just head over to the cash register, where the photographer who took your photos will be waiting to take photos of you *buying* your photos. But instead of trying to sell you *those* photos, he'll simply try to get you to buy him a new camera after you've smashed his old one over his head with enough fury to make Sean Penn proud.

Chapter 8: Getting Settled

Getting into Your Cabin

Most cruise ships start embarkation between 11 a.m. and noon and set sail between 3 p.m. and 4 p.m. What most first-time cruisers don't realize is that you won't be able to get into your cabin until around 1 p.m. This is because the Housekeeping Department's team members need ample time to clean up your cabin after the previous residents. With all the eating, partying, humping and fighting the previous cruise's inhabitants engaged in, your cabin will need to be stripped, scrubbed, fumigated, disinfected, sterilized, painted and hermetically sealed for your protection. It will *need* to be. Unfortunately, all your cabin steward *will* do is change the sheets, replace the towels and run the vacuum a few feet in every direction. The reason this will take until one or two in the afternoon is that, due to budget cuts, there are only three or four Indonesians to clean every cabin on the entire ship. (And they're all named "Putu," which, in Indonesian, means "Gary.")

Complaining to Guest Services

The most fun you'll have on your cruise by far will be going down to Guest Services and complaining about stupid stuff so you can get free stuff. By doing whatever they can to mollify dissatisfied passengers, cruise lines have taught perfectly satisfied passengers to manufacture complaints purely for compensation. But just because you're an honest and grateful person whose strong moral compass prevents you from nitpicking for dubious financial gain doesn't mean you should miss out on all the fun. So here are a few complaints to get you started:

Five Starter Cruise Ship Complaints for Beginners

1. "The curtains were open in my cabin and so I was blinded by the sunlight. Now I'm going to need cornea

surgery when I get home. I demand a free cruise or at least a half-off drink coupon."

2. "My cabin isn't the same color as the one I saw on your website. That cabin had beige décor and mine has blue. I'm allergic to blue and now my body is covered with hives, especially the parts covered by the blue shorts and tank top I'm currently wearing. And so since I'm not going to be able to leave my cabin, I demand a free cruise or at least a plate of chocolate-covered strawberries. Chocolate is brown and strawberries are red, so I'll be fine; but, the plate better not be blue or I'm going to switch to Royal Caribbean—even though their logo is blue."

3. "I don't like the background music playing in the hallways. Instrumental versions of Beatles classics flood me with an overwhelming sense of melancholy and ennui. I demand a free cruise or at least one of those cool lanyards you give VIP gamblers in the casino."

4. "It's too hot outside and too cold inside. I demand a free cruise on the same ship during the same time of the year because, although it's too cold inside and too hot outside *now*, if the cruise were free, then I could easily put on a sweatshirt when I'm inside and then take it off when I'm outside. If I can't get a free cruise, then I'd like one of those official sweatshirts for sale in your gift shop. I'd pay for it but it's even colder inside the gift shop than it is here in the lobby so I might get hypothermia and die, in which case I'll have to sue this cruise line for every last penny. So if I were you, I'd just give me the sweatshirt. But just make sure it's not too warm."

5. "I'm diabetic—I think—and yet my cabin steward left a chocolate candy on my pillow. I suspect that this is an attempt to send me into diabetic shock so I will have to be airlifted to the local hospital so you can sell my cabin as an upgrade to somebody else. I demand either a free

45

cruise or a free bag of chocolate candy from the gift shop."

No, really. If you truly want to have fun on your cruise, don't spend your days lounging around the pool or relaxing at the bar. Instead, make frequent trips down to Guest Services and complain about anything that comes to mind. If your complaints are inventive enough, the ship's Guest Services associates will often offer you financial compensation just to shut you up. If you're unlucky enough to cruise on an awesome ship like mine, however, you'll be hard-pressed to find many legitimate issues to complain about. In that case, here are some advanced complaints for stepping up your game:

Five Advanced Cruise Ship Complaints for Real Assholes—I mean—Expert Cruisers

1. "The sound of the ocean keeps me up at night. Can you turn it off?"
2. "It's too hot on the open decks. Can you ask the Captain to turn on the air conditioning outside?"
3. "It's too long of a walk up the stairs between decks. Can you shorten your steps?"
4. "The midnight buffet is too late at night. Can you reschedule it for noon?"
5. "I hate discos and disco music. Yet every time I go into the disco all I hear is *disco* music. Can I have a free cruise? Or at least a couple of free Bee Gees CDs?"

Getting Your Luggage and Unpacking

When the porter takes your luggage at the pier, he'll tell you that your luggage will be delivered directly to your cabin by six o'clock in the evening. Ignore him. When you check in at the terminal, the person checking you in will tell you that your luggage will be delivered to your cabin by six o'clock. Ignore her. When you step off the gangway and into the lobby of the ship, the band will be playing a song called, "Your Luggage Will Be Delivered to Your Cabin by Six o'Clock." When you actually arrive at your cabin around two in the afternoon to throw your carry-on bags onto the bed and then freshen up a bit, your cabin steward will greet you in the hallway, look you in the eyes and, in perfect English, tell you *that your luggage will be delivered to your cabin by six o'clock.* Fortunately, since it's only two o'clock, you now have four hours to sit on the edge of your bed and call Guest Services every five minutes to ask where the hell your luggage is.

Chapter 9: Exploring the Ship

The Lobby

If you have any energy left after your complaint marathon, you can take a brief tour of the ship. The first stop should be the lobby, which is usually a beehive of activity, beautifully decorated, and the centerpiece for the ship's overall interior decoration theme. The purpose of the lobby's dazzling design is to have you looking up at the walls and ceilings in awe at all the beautiful and ornate decorations so you can trip over all the empty drink glasses and beer bottles your fellow guests have left on the floor. Luckily, there'll be a photographer nearby to take your picture before you even hit the ground.

The Spa

Once you make it past the phalanx of photographers in the lobby, you'll be handed a stack of flyers for the ship's spa by one of their "Spa Girls." These charming, pretty and ubiquitous young ladies will offer you "special embark day prices" on the following spa treatments:

- Total body massage - $200 per hour (normally $1,000 per hour)
- Foot massage - $100 per foot (normally whatever the limit on your credit card is)
- Relaxing facial - $75 (which is usually the price for the *stress-inducing* facial)
- Scalp massage – Free with any overpriced haircut
- Acupuncture - $1 per needle (5,000 needle minimum)

If you're wondering why the discounted prices for popular on-board spa treatments still seem kind of pricey, it probably has something to do with the expense involved with handing out thousands of flyers every day to overweight and out-of-shape cruise ship passengers who are ultimately either just going to toss them in the garbage or else slather them with mustard and try to eat them.

In addition to a full-service gym complete with a sauna and steam room, most cruise ship spas offer health and fitness seminars designed to help you regain your health and lose weight. The most popular of these seminars is called, "For Starters—Don't Go on a Cruise!"

Promenade Deck

The Promenade Deck, or main drag, is where all the action is. On most ships, the Promenade Deck features the gift shop, candy shop, coffee shop, casino, beer pubs and specialty restaurants such as a steakhouse or sushi bar. The Promenade is usually bright and sparkly and filled with music, noise and bright, twinkly lights. The ambience is usually one of class and luxury made even classier and more luxurious by your fellow cruisers, who are walking around shirtless and shoeless in wet bathing suits, dripping water and melted ice cream everywhere so you can start your cruise off by slipping, falling and breaking your neck.

The Gift Shop

The ship's gift shop is where you'll find unbelievable deals on high-end watches, jewelry, and, after slipping and falling on Promenade Deck, neck braces.

Some guests cruise specifically to buy precious gemstones at prices you simply cannot find on land. One of the most popular gemstones nowadays is Tanzanite, a stone so rare you can only find it on every single cruise ship ever built. It's called Tanzanite because it's mined on the planet Tanzania, at the far end of the Milky Way. I know Tanzanite is rare because that's what all cruise ship gift shop sales associates say.

Your gift shop sales associates will tell you that you won't find better prices in the jewelry stores in the upcoming ports of call. Of course this is the exact opposite of what you'll hear from the ship's shopping specialist, because he or she will tell you that certain stores in port will offer the ship's passengers the best deals on land or sea. Some of the more upscale ships will often schedule UFC cage matches pitting the gift shop manager against the shopping specialist and air them in your cabin on pay-per-view.

The Casino

Pretty much every cruise line except Disney makes a good share of its profits from its on-board casinos. Neither the odds against winning big nor the absence of the usual complimentary cocktails gamers score in Vegas or Atlantic City keep guests from trying their luck at the one-armed bandits, the roulette wheel or the poker tables. One of the ships I worked on had a brand new BMW on display in the casino. Supposedly, guests could have won the BMW while playing a special progressive slot machine. But, as guests made one one-dollar spin after another, it never occurred to them to ask, "What are the odds the cruise line is going to want to go through the trouble of getting this car back off the ship?"

My current ship has a giant photo of a previous guest holding up a check for $5,000. Proof that anyone—maybe even *you*—can win a slot machine jackpot. Sure, $5,000 is a lot of money; just not a lot of money to win in a casino, considering how many thousands of guests leave the ship every week thousands of dollars down. Oh sure, there may have been several bigger winners since then; the cruise line just doesn't want to spend the money to take a new photo.

Another great thing about the casino is you'll meet lots of interesting people who do very interesting things, such as drop a couple of grand at the blackjack table like it's chump change and then take their cabin stewards' gratuity off their bills.

The Nightclub

If your idea of a relaxing night out is listening to sexually explicit gangsta rap played at ear-splitting levels and watching drunken college kids dirty dance while the DJ interrupts every three minutes to announce, "Please no drinks on the dance floor!" then the ship's nightclub—or "dance club" or "disco"—is waiting for you. Most cruise lines have strict guidelines for what genre of dance music—and sometimes specific songs—the DJ can play. Of course, nobody ever tells the DJ this or, if they do, he's too deaf to hear.

Lido Deck

The center of outdoor activity, Lido Deck is home of the pool, poolside bars, 24-hour pizza and, on some ships, a movie-screen-sized television showing blockbuster movies (*Titanic*), electrifying concerts (Olivia Newton John), and riveting sporting events (championship cricket). The most fun thing to do on Lido Deck is trying to find an empty deck chair; because, no matter what time of day you go to Lido Deck, every deck chair has a beach towel, T-shirt, sandal or some other personal effect on it, signaling that that particular deck chair is being saved by its current occupant, who is usually back home already, planning her next cruise.

The Medical Center

Every cruise ship as a fully equipped and fully staffed medical center, where doctors and nurses will be ready to treat you for just about any illness or injury. The important thing to remember is that no matter what you need medical attention for, be sure to blame the cruise line for it so you that can avoid having to pay for your treatment. For example, if you get drunk and trip down the stairs, blame the cruise line for making their mojitos so damn tasty. If you have a heart attack, blame the cruise line for telling you how much those mojitos cost. If you get hemorrhoids, blame them for letting you spend the entire cruise drunk on mojitos, complaining about anything and everything, without their once ever telling you to pull your head out of your ass.

Chapter 10: Expecting the Unexpected

Your Closet—I Mean, Cabin

The surest way to be disappointed on a cruise is to expect everything to be perfect. The ship will be nice. The service will be good. The food will be decent. But keep in mind that your ship, even if only a few years old, is a vessel visited by over 3,000 different people week after week, so just as the Tom Cruise you run into at Whole Foods has more wrinkles and blemishes than the Tom Cruise you see up on the silver screen, your ship is not going to be as bright and shiny as in the TV commercials. (But at least your ship won't try to recruit you into Scientology.)

Let's start with your cabin. The first thing you'll need to remember is that you're on a ship, not in a hotel. Your cabin, even if it's one of the snazzier ones, will likely be smaller than you imagined. Even if you splurge on an ocean-view cabin, don't expect your balcony to be a sprawling deck complete with patio furniture from IKEA. The balcony will be small. The bathroom will be small. The beds will small. The hallway will be noisy. The guests in the cabin next to yours will be noisy. You'll be woken up by stupid announcements from Guest Services and the cruise director. But still, the room will be clean and cozy. And remember that your cabin steward works long days and has lots of cabins to clean so he might miss some small things here and there, such as a dead body in the bathtub. (Just kidding. There are no bathtubs on cruise ships. Dead bodies go under the bed.)

The coolest thing in your cabin will definitely be the toilet. Because if you ever get tired of your cruise and want to leave the ship immediately, all you have to do is flush while sitting down. Although I'm not sure why, all cruise ship toilets create enough air pressure while flushing to send a fully grown adult back to Kansas without having to wait for a wizard and his balloon.

Long Lines

Yes, cruising is exciting. Yes, cruising is fun. But relaxing? Not so sure about that one. I mean, sure, you'll be much more relaxed then you are at work; but, how much can you really, truly relax when you're surrounded by people *everywhere*? Cruise ships contain a *whole lot* of people. And where there are people there are lines. Again, this is why they call them cruise *lines*. There'll be...

- A line to get on the shuttle bus
- A line to get off the shuttle bus
- A line to check in at the terminal
- A line to go through terminal security
- A line to board the ship
- A line to buy your soft drink or alcoholic beverages discount card
- A line to book your shore excursions
- A line to request a different dinner seating time
- A line to complain at Guests Services
- A line to eat in the buffet restaurant
- A line to get into the formal dining room
- A line to get your picture taken
- A line to pay for your pictures
- A line to pay for your items in the gift shops
- A line to check-out towels at the pool
- A line to get late-night pizza
- A line to watch the comedian in the comedy club
- A line to kick the comedian's ass for making fun of you for wearing a tank top and flip-flops on formal night

And, if lines make you so stressed out and angry that you think you're going to explode, then Guest Services associates are there to listen closely and sympathetically to your complaints. All you have to do is march straight down to Guest Services and *get in line*, beotch.

Kids, Kids and More Kids

If your main reason for going on a cruise is to get away from your kids for a week, make sure you pick the right week. If you go during summer vacation, winter holidays or spring break, you'll be trading *your* kids for *other people's* kids. And, after watching them charge around the ship with no supervision, knocking over old ladies with walkers, crashing into waiters balancing huge trays of $9 drinks, and cannon balling pool water onto your Kindle, you'll wish you had brought your kids along just so they can throw those little Grandsons of Anarchy a beating.

Although most ships have one or more kids' clubs that keep the little angels occupied during the day, the nighttime is when they grow their fangs and sprout their demon wings. If you've cruised before, you may have observed them in the hallways, on the stairwells or in the elevator lobbies well past midnight: gangs of preteens roaming the ship like miniature marauders—laughing and shouting, blasting Justin Bieber or Miley Cyrus on their iPhones without headphones, riding the elevators up and down for no reason, and just plain annoying the hell out of anyone unlucky enough not to own a tranquilizer gun with a laser sight. Sure, you can call Security, but Security will always say the same thing: "Sorry, sir (even if you're a woman), but we asked those kids if they were causing trouble and they said, 'No'."

Although teenagers and preteens can be loud and obnoxious, a disapproving stare is usually enough to calm them down. It's the *little* kids with no "off" switches who'll drive you crazy. Cruise at the wrong time of year and you'll be surrounded by sugar-crazed kiddies hijacking the ship like little preschool pirates. Kiddies screeching in the dining room. Kiddies crying in the comedy club. Kiddies peeing in the hot tub. Kiddies looking innocently up at you with cute, excited little faces just as you're about ready to kick them down a flight of stairs, causing you to pat them on the head, instead, and say, "See that elderly couple quietly playing cards in the corner? Go screech near *them!*"

Even though I love children and am used to them wreaking havoc on my ship, my fantasies of punting them overboard never last more than a second or two, long enough for me to imagine what I'd rather do to their parents, instead, should I find them. (Which is unlikely, because the majority of parents remove their children's leashes at the beginning of the cruise, never to see their demon spawn again until reclaiming them on the luggage carousel in the terminal at the end of the cruise.)

As the cousin of a parent of two wonderfully behaved youngsters who managed to enjoy their first cruise on my ship immensely while causing no trouble whatsoever, I can testify that it's possible for kids to have the time of their lives without ruining the cruise for adults.

Unfortunately, my cousin and her husband were fined heavily by my cruise line for their children's exemplary behavior. Apparently, the Home Office feels that well-behaved kids risk ruining the fun vacation atmosphere we're known for. That's why every parent is supposed to receive a "Complete Idiot's Guide to Being a Complete Idiot: Cruise Ship Parenting 101" pamphlet that helps children enjoy their cruise more than the grownups who actually paid for it.

"Complete Idiot's Guide to Being a Complete Idiot: Cruise Ship Parenting 101"

1. **Never know where your kids are.** And, if they're stampeding around the ship unattended, yelling, screaming and disturbing other passengers, do not stop them. Just because a crew member has chastised them multiple times doesn't mean this conduct is unacceptable. In fact, get that crew member's name

because you can bet it's been a while since your captain has made someone walk the plank.

2. **The public restrooms are for grownups,** so if your kids have to pee, that's what the "adults-only" hot tub is for.

3. **Do not ask your children to say "please" or "thank you"** when being served in the dining room. "Honey Boo-Boo" never learned table manners so what makes your kids so special?

4. **Sit irritable or rambunctious toddlers in the front row of the comedy show.** The only thing comedians love more than a drunken heckler sitting two feet from the stage is a wailing or fidgeting rug rat sitting two feet from the stage and stepping on the drunken heckler's punchlines.

5. **If a show in the main theater isn't suitable for your tiny tots, drag them along anyway.** Having them play distracting computer games on a tablet or whine "Mommy, I'm bored!" for an hour straight will force the passengers seated around you to pay better attention to the show, thereby enjoying it more.

6. **Show zero respect for the ship's property.** If you catch your child doing something you would never tolerate in your own home, such as yanking down on the lever of the frozen yogurt machine until its entire contents swirl into a messy mound on the floor, be sure to laugh your head off and then snap a photo for your Instagram account.

So the next time you want a break from your kids, don't go on a cruise—go to Chuck E. Cheese. It'll be much quieter and the pizza will be better.

Expensive Drinks

It costs a lot of money to run a cruise ship. First, there's the fuel. The ship I work on weighs over 100,000 tons, so it costs around three quarters of a million dollars to fill her up every week.

Then there are 4,500 guests we have to feed and entertain. And 1,500 crew members to feed, clothe (uniforms), pay, and provide medical care for. Because your base fare doesn't even begin to pay for the overhead of a bustling mega liner, there are plenty of ways that cruise lines make up for it: the casino, the gift shop, shore excursions, spa treatments and—yes, you guessed it—bar sales. Alcohol offers the highest profit margin, especially the "drink of the day." Even though cruise ship drinks are made much stronger than on land—water down the drinks on a cruise ship and you'll have a mutiny on your hands—most of them are premade in huge batches for a small fraction of the advertised menu price. On my ship, the going price for a 16-ounce Long Island Iced Tea is $9. Drinks like that are made in batches with well liquor so the profit margin is ridiculous. You get drunk on half a drink, so you're happy. And then you keep buying the next one and then next one because you're too drunk to realize how much money you're spending, so now the cruise line's happy. (Ordinarily, I wouldn't give away trade secrets like this, but I'm really drunk right now.)

Tender Ports

When a port lacks a pier large enough to accommodate cruise ships, it's called a "tender port." A "tender" is a boat that takes you from the ship to the port in the time it would take you to swim. Tendering is lots of fun because you get to wake up early, report to one of the ship's lounges with hundreds of other tired and impatient guests, and wait for hours on end, watching CNN on the big screen with the sound off (so you can hear all the screeching babies and screaming toddlers sprawled out around you) until you decide to jump overboard and swim ashore.

Once on dry land, you'll be free to slouch around in the scorching heat for 10 minutes, trying to find a discount T-shirt shop with functioning air conditioning until you finally realize that you're in a Third-World country that doesn't really have all that much to see or do so you might as well get in line for a tender back to the ship, where you can be laughed at by all the experienced cruisers who stayed on board.

Dangerous Ports

You can read all the online articles you want about the crime and violence in popular ports of call such as St. Thomas and Jamaica, but I'm here to remind you that St. Thomas, for one, is actually part of America. That means it's no more dangerous than, say, Camden, New Jersey.

But just because some ports have dangerous areas doesn't mean anything's going to happen to *you.* Sure, you *might* get shot or stabbed at an ATM, but at least you'll have pretty coconut trees to look up at while you're lying on the ground, bleeding to death.

Jamaica, coincidentally, is where Angela Basset filmed the movie *How Stella Got Her Groove Back.* I can't remember exactly how Stella got her groove back, but I *can* tell you how she *lost* it: Stella left her groove in the trunk of a rental car in Montego Bay and that groove got *jacked*, Jack.

I wasn't prepared for how filthy parts of Jamaica are, either. Litter everywhere. Then again, with as much ganja that's smoked in that country (travel agents *love* Jamaica, mon), I guess it shouldn't be much of a surprise to see thousands of candy wrappers blowing in the breeze. If you ask me, we should give our ship's entire Housekeeping Department the morning off in Montego Bay. They'd have that whole city spic and span in three hours and still be back in time to clean up after our messy-ass passengers before lunch.

All jokes aside, if you go exploring in Caribbean ports, make sure you travel with a large group of other tourists. You'll fell a lot less frightened and intimidated if you're not the only person being robbed at gunpoint.

Most islanders will sneer at American travel advisories. They'll ask how we can call their port cities dangerous when

America has Cleveland and Detroit. I'll keep that in mind the next time I drop two grand on a seven-day cruise around Lake Erie.

The other problem with crime in the Caribbean is that criminals are rarely caught. It's easier to catch the Zika virus than a purse snatcher. There was more justice in 1964 Selma than in modern day Honduras, for example. Of the last 50 Americans killed in Honduras, the local police have solved just two cases. Their top detectives determined that one victim was killed by a murderer and the other was murdered by a killer.

Because a forewarned traveler is a safe(er) traveler, here's...

The Fun Dude's Top 10 List of Ports to Watch Your Ass in:

1. **St. Lucia:** Armed robberies are so common on this island that a local tour company offers a shore excursion that enables you to ride around the city in a tour bus and watch actual crimes in progress, giving new meaning to the phrase, "mugging for the camera."
2. **El Salvador:** El Salvador has one of the highest murder rates in the world. But, then again, you can get a wicked mango daiquiri for dirt cheap. So don't let anybody scare you out of getting your drink on.
3. **United States Virgin Islands (USVI):** The U.S. Virgin islands are filled with so many guns, drugs and robberies, that most Americans should feel right at home.
4. **Antigua:** Although Antigua may seem like a tropical paradise, it's seen more than its share of tragedies. For example, Justin Bieber vacationed there once and nothing happened to him.
5. **St. Kitts:** James Bond refuses to go there anymore ever since he walked outside his hotel and found his Aston Martin up on blocks.
6. **Mexico:** Kidnappings and beheadings don't usually happen in the tourist areas, which makes seeing one at the Hard Rock Café in Acapulco that much more special.

7. **Guatemala:** Guatemala is not a place where you should think of going for a leisurely stroll through the back streets. You'd be better off rollerblading straight into—and then straight outta—Compton.
8. **Venezuela:** Venezuela also has one of the highest murder rates. One American cruise passenger was killed simply for wearing a fanny pack. (So at least that guy had it coming.)
9. **Honduras:** Like many other Caribbean islands, the police are either corrupt or incompetent. So this is where big-city police departments from the States come down every spring to scout new recruits.
10. **Bahamas:** The U.S. State Department has issued numerous crime warnings for the Bahamas. The second you step off the cruise ship you're likely to be offered drugs. Fortunately, those drugs will most likely be Lipitor and Viagra, so at least Bahamian drug dealers know their market.

Minimizing Your Risks

Here are some safety measures you can take to reduce the risk of becoming a crime victim while on vacation:

- Travel in groups of two or more. Never get into a taxi with a passenger already inside, even when offered a chance to split the fare. The driver and the "passenger" may be in cahoots. The way to tell if your taxi driver is for real is to ask if he has change for a twenty. If he says, "Yes," he's not a real taxi driver.
- Keep a low profile. You can achieve this by either dressing inconspicuously or by signing up for a My Space account.
- Do not wear a fanny pack (especially in Venezuela). If you don't wind up being robbed of your money, you'll be robbed of your dignity.
- Never put valuable items in a backpack, unless you're a man and it's a "Hello Kitty" backpack, in which case your

61

assailants will be too busy mocking you to actually rob you.

- Moreover, men, never carry your billfold in your back pocket. Samuel L. Jackson isn't the only person who wants to know what's in your wallet. I recommend carrying a trick novelty wallet that shoots out a fake rubber serpent. That way, if Samuel L. Jackson himself ever asks you what's in your wallet, you can open it in his face and shout, "Mother-@#$-ing snakes—that's what's in my mother-@#$-ing wallet, beotch!"

- If you're a woman, don't carry your purse over your shoulder; carry it across your chest. This will cause your would-be purse snatcher to focus on your boobs instead of your purse.

- Money belts are for amateurs. Nothing says "easy mark" to a pickpocket like taking your shirt off to buy a Snickers bar.

- Take just one or two credit cards and a small amount of cash ashore with you in order to minimize your losses in case a thief gets you in his sights. Better yet, max out all your cards out at home, before you leave for your cruise.

- Unless absolutely unavoidable, never go ashore with your actual passport; bring a photocopy of the data pages. If Guest Services won't let you use their photocopier on the ship, you can use one at the local police station in port while reporting your stolen wallet.

- Which reminds me: carry a "mugger's wallet." This is a cheap decoy wallet with a small amount of cash inside and that you'll find in your pocket after realizing that you gave the mugger your actual wallet by mistake.

- Leave your cell phone in your cabin. Expensive smartphones, such as an iPhone or Galaxy, are the most common items stolen from cruise-ship passengers. If you need to make a call, you can always steal a phone from a fellow tourist.

- Most important, try to stay sober. The drunker you are, the more likely ransom-hungry kidnappers are to mistake you for Lindsay Lohan.

Although I do want you to think before gallivanting around a Third-World island nation with a fancy camera around your neck, I don't mean to scare you into scrubbing your cruise plans. As I made clear at the start of this chapter, sailing around the Caribbean isn't any more dangerous than biking through Baltimore and then catching a ride with the Police in the back of a paddy wagon with no seat belts.

So, if you exercise caution, stay aware of your surroundings, and don't venture too far off the beaten path, you'll be able to party your ass off without losing it or getting it kicked.

Chapter 11: Enjoying the Safety Briefing

Muster Stations

Before your ship can set sail you'll have to attend a passenger safety briefing, otherwise known as a "boat drill." This is a perfect opportunity to show all the foreign crew members who'll be assisting in the drill how superior Americans are to other nationalities. While the Indonesians, Filipinos, South Americans, South Africans and Eastern Europeans with emergency station duties are trying to teach you important survival information that could save your life in the event of an actual emergency, you can show them how Americans laugh in the face of danger by talking on your phone, sorting through your photos, Tweeting, and updating your Facebook status.

Anyone who has ever cruised before is familiar with the boat drill. Vacation fun is put on hold as the ship's officers close the bars and order passengers to gather at an assigned meeting place for a lesson on how to don a life jacket (by *putting it on*) and what to do in case of an emergency (start talking on your phone, sorting through your photos, Tweeting and updating your Facebook status).

Life Jackets

The most important thing you're going to learn at the safety briefing is how to don your life jacket. Your first instinct will be to *put on* your life jacket. Instead, you want to *don* it. Putting it on wouldn't require any instruction. Just *putting on* a life jacket is easy. You just put it over your head, wrap the strap around your back and then buckle the strap. But to *don* a life jacket is a completely different process. To don a life jacket—as opposed to putting it on—you must put the lifejacket over your head, wrap the strap around your pack and then buckle the strap. This is a completely different process and requires watching a bored, overworked crew member demonstrate the various steps in front of you while you sort through your photos, Tweet, and update your Facebook status.

Every lifejacket has reflective patches, a light and a whistle. The light and patches are for being seen in the dark or from a distance and the whistle is so you can catch GI from the person who was playing around with it last week.

Part 3: Meeting the Crew

Chapter 12: Cabin Stewards

Hardest Job on the Ship

The hardest job on the ship belongs to your cabin—or stateroom, if you're an elitist douche—steward. Your steward is responsible for keeping your cabin clean and comfortable. He'll make your bed, arrange your toiletries, exchange your towels, restock your mini bar, bring you fresh ice, have your dress clothes pressed, and leave adorable towel animals on your bed that will scare the crap out of you when you stumble into your cabin drunk at 3 a.m. He'll also vacuum the hallway outside your door at 6 a.m. while chattering with his colleagues in Indonesian, Spanish or Tagalog. Then, when you poke your head out into the hallway to politely ask if he can hold off on the vacuuming until you can introduce a few gallons of coffee into your bloodstream, he'll hand you breakfast on a tray with one hand while combing your hair with the other.

What most first-time cruisers don't realize at first is that the average stateroom—because I'm an elitist douche, too—steward is responsible for maintaining between 30 and 40 cabins daily. On top of that, he may be asked to help out in the public areas for an hour or two on his "breaks." And, on debark/embark day, all stewards must help out with the offloading and loading of guest luggage. This takes anywhere from four to eight hours and is in addition to readying all 30 or so of their cabins for a new batch of guests. There are 9-year-olds in a Chinese tennis shoe factory right now thinking, "Thank Buddha I don't work on a cruise ship!"

Not only will your steward or stewardess (cruise lines don't discriminate when it comes to overworking people) give you outstanding service, he'll do so with a smile. Cabin stewards work the longest hours on the ship and yet are somehow always smiling and in a good mood. Unfortunately, not everyone can appreciate this amazing display of character. Believe it or not, many guests opt to have their stewards' automatic gratuities removed from their bills. In fact, you can learn a lot about yourself by how you view your cabin steward's efforts during your cruise. If you are humbled by his hard work and find yourself bringing him cookies from the buffet, chatting him up about his life back home, keeping your cabin as clean as possible so as not to make extra work for him, and finally giving him an extra tip at the end of the cruise, you can rest assured that you're a good person. But if, instead, you find yourself thinking, *Hey—that's what he gets for not finding a better job back home in his country. So what if his job is hard? He should have known that going into this. There's no way I'm tipping him extra. I paid a thousand dollars to be on this ship so housekeeping service should be included. Why should I tip him extra just for doing his job? Nobody tips* me *for doing* my *job. Is it my problem if cruise-ship workers frequently have to pay hundreds if not thousands of dollars for training, pre-employment physical exams, plane tickets, and recruiters' fees?* then this means you're simply the average American, so I wouldn't worry about it if I were you.

Another thing new cruisers don't realize is that proper housekeeping is a learned skill. Indonesians and Filipinos aren't born with mops in their hands. In fact, they don't even have cleaning supplies in Indonesia and the Philippines. People there just leave their windows open and wait for a typhoon to tidy up after them.

On a cruise ship, somebody is always cleaning something somewhere. But just like waiters and cooks, all cabin stewardesses must start at the bottom during their first contracts and learn their trade from scratch. Before your stewardess can have the pleasure of cleaning your guest cabin, she has to work hard cleaning the public areas of the ships—everything from stacking deck chairs to draining the swimming pools, polishing the handrails and wiping the ice-cream-streaked windows of the glass elevators. That's why before she can clean guest areas, your stewardess has to spend several months cleaning officer cabins. And before she can spend several months cleaning officer cabins, she has to spend several months cleaning staff cabins. And before she can spend several months cleaning staff cabins, she has to spend several months cleaning crew cabins. And before she can spend several months cleaning crew cabins, she has to spend several months cleaning crew public areas. And before she can spend several months cleaning crew public areas, she has to spend a lifetime back in her home country stepping over dead bodies in the street.

As you can see, there's a lot of training and dues paying involved in becoming a cabin steward or stewardess. My steward, who does an amazing job, is chomping at the bit to get promoted up to guest cabins, so the other day he said to me, "Mr. Fun Dude, am I doing a good job for you? I would like to be promoted so I can send more money back home to my family in Bali."

"Gary (Putu)," I said, "For somebody who is thousands of miles from home, working for an American company for the first time, in a second language, cleaning fifty to sixty cabins all by himself from six in the morning until ten at night with only eight hours off each day—anytime spent eating, relaxing or showering cuts into your eight hours of sleep—and no time to watch TV, no time to go into the ports, no time to play pool, no time to read— just work, work, work, sixteen hours a day, every day of the week, with no days off, for up to thirteen months at a time? For someone like *that*—I expected much more from you, buddy."

The Language Barrier

Fortunately, all crew members on the major American cruise lines are required to speak perfect English. Unfortunately for them, you, the guest, are not. Although you're new to cruising, you're probably also an American, which means you probably automatically expect every foreigner you meet to speak English. So on your first cruise you'll no doubt mumble at light speed to your cabin steward, expecting him to grasp every tasty nuance of your stammering soliloquies. You'll use slang, advanced idioms, inside jokes and a regional accent—and yet he'll laugh and smile and nod his head after everything you say, leading you to believe that he possesses an uncanny mastery of American English. Until, that is, you ask him for a bucket of ice and he brings you an orange.

You see, just because your steward *speaks* English perfectly doesn't mean he *understands* English perfectly, especially not the kind of hyper-caffeinated, anxiety-riddled, haven't-had-a-vacation-in-a-decade English you probably speak. The best way to circumvent the language barrier on a cruise ship is to speak slowly and clearly, and to eschew all slang and idiomatic language, as well as fancy words such as "eschew." Then, ask your steward to repeat what you said back to you so you can be sure that he understands you. Because most cabin stewards come from cultures where it's considered impolite to ask somebody to speak more slowly or to repeat herself, your steward will most likely pretend to understand you no matter what you say. So, if you say, "Hey buddy, I am totally spent after a brutal flight and am so dang ravenous I could eat the ass end of a hog. Let me wash off the funk, throw on some jams and head up to Lido Deck to toss a little grub down my gullet. As soon as I vamoose, you can waltz on in and do your thang, my good man, you feel me?" He'll smile, bow his head and say "Yes, yes. Right away, right away." You'll feel exceedingly proud of your uncanny ability to powwow with the natives until he returns two minutes later with a toilet plunger and a tambourine.

Towel Animals

Every night, while you're at dinner, your cabin steward will turn down your bed and then leave a towel animal on it. A towel animal is created by folding bath towels—just like origami except with towels instead of paper. Some common towel animals are elephants, frogs, bears, monkeys, rabbits and swans. Sometimes, your steward will leave you a snake, which is basically one towel rolled up like a giant joint (travel agents go crazy for this one). This is your steward's way of telling you that he's tired of your leaving your dirty underwear on the floor.

Chapter 13: Guest Services

Complaints R Us

The second hardest job on the ship belongs to the hard-working guys and gals down at Guest Services. These folks, previously known as "pursers," are at the front desk around the clock, making sure that your on-board experience is everything it's supposed to be. And the great thing is that these people are not Americans, so you don't have to adhere to the same rules of good manners and decorum that apply when dealing with customer service representatives in America. For example, if you have a problem with shoddy car repairs, you'll want to make sure to keep your temper in check at the dealership so they don't decide to seriously screw up your car even more. Or complain too loudly in an American restaurant on land and the chef will drag his "rolling pin" through your entrée.

On a ship, however, you're in international waters, talking to non-Americans—so, time to flex those pecs and let it fly, baby. Part of you might instinctively want to behave as nicely as possible in order to get the Guest Services associate on your side and *want* to help you, but why waste your time and energy? These folks are from foreign countries where magic is part of daily life; however, this magic can only be unlocked if you throw an embarrassing, infantile hissy fit. If Petra from Slovakia tells you that there are no more ocean-view cabins to move you into, all you need to do is yell and scream at her and then another open cabin number will automatically appear on her computer screen. If you've been told that your luggage won't be in your cabin until 6 p.m., just walk up to Ivan from Serbia, pound your fist on the counter and shout, "It's three-thirty in the afternoon—where the hell is my luggage?!" Then watch in amazement as Ivan presses a special button on his desk and your luggage magically shoots out of his ass and lands at your feet.

No Americans Allowed

One of the first things guests ask me is, "What's an American like you doing working as a crew member on a cruise ship?"

My stock answer is: "I'm not a crew member. I'm actually the president of the cruise line, taping an episode of 'Undercover Boss'."

My backup joke is: "My last boss was a real jerk so I told him he could take that job on shove it. And this where you end up when you do stupid crap like that."

Almost every American team member on my ship works in the Entertainment Department. My cruise line learned the hard way that we Americans are much more entertaining than, say, Croatians: "OK, everybody, it is time to play da trivias: 'What country is so stupid dey turned 'Here Comes Honey Boo' into a ratings bonanza?' Dat's right: America. You win—have another Twinkie, Fatso!"

And, as I mentioned before, very few American staff members work in Guest Services. That's because most cruise lines realize that sarcasm doesn't play well with weary travelers:

FIRST-TIME CRUISER:

"Excuse me, but do I have to pay for those items in my mini bar?"

AMERICAN GUEST SERVICES ASSOCIATE:

"Of course not, madam, we're a cruise line. Why would we buy a bag at M & M's at Wal-Mart for twenty-five cents and then charge you seven dollars for them when you stumble back drunk and depressed from the casino at three o'clock in the morning?"

VIP GUEST:

"Excuse me, but there's a whooshing and slamming sound coming from my cabin wall at night and it's keeping me awake."

AMERICAN GUEST SERVICES ASSOCIATE:

"Yes, sir, that would be the sound of the ocean."

VIP GUEST:

"Well, hell, can you make it stop?"

AMERICAN GUEST SERVICES ASSOCIATE:

"Yes, sir, I will call the captain and ask him to pop a wheelie all the way to our next port."

The amazing thing about the folks down at Guest Services is they can handle just about anything you throw at them. No matter the nature of your complaint, they're required to open a report, document your concerns, offer a solution, and then follow up.

For example, if you were to complain about a bartender putting a too-small slice of pineapple on the rim of your pricey piña colada, as soon as you were to get back to your cabin, a Filipino would be waiting at your door with a 50-pound pineapple wedge on a trolley. "This is free gift for you," he'd say. "Pineapple this big keep your mouth busy so you can't bitch no more."

The best thing about cruising is you can leave your dirty dishes wherever you want and no one will say a thing.

At least not in English.

But listen closely and you'll learn to say "lazy American" in 50 foreign languages.

In fact, that's the real reason you won't see many American crew members on a cruise ship. Most cruise lines realize that if a foreign crew member sees you leave a dirty dish on the staircase, he'll pick it up for you. But if an *American* crew member sees you leave a dirty dish in the middle of the stairs, he'll say, "Really, Bubba?! *That's* where you're going to leave it? Where some nice old lady can trip, fall and break her neck right in front of her grandchildren?! Shame on you, you lazy slob—pick that crap up and put it on that counter ten feet from your fat ass before I slap some sense into you the way your mama should have thirty years ago!"

So the next time you find yourself on a cruise ship, feeling more important than the other 4,000 passengers on board, be glad the crew doesn't understand English well enough to argue with you.

One of the fun things I find about living and working alongside crew members from all around the world is teaching them about the American political process during an election year. My cabin steward said to me, "Mr. Fun Dude, will you please explain the differences between the main political parties in America for me?"

I said, "Sure thing, Putu (Gary). Let's say your city is having a problem controlling the local deer population. Republicans will tell you to shoot the deer. Democrats will tell you to give the deer free condoms. The Tea Party will tell you to convert the deer to Christianity. Libertarians will tell you to leave the deer alone, and then run the craziest deer in the herd as their candidate. Meanwhile, Donald Trump will be on CNN, promising to build a wall around the deer before deporting them back to the Third-World petting zoo they came from."

Chapter 14: Dining Room Waiters

Ship Food

I read that the average American male weighs 190 pounds, whereas the average American female weighs 160 pounds. This proves what I've been saying for years: the guests on my ship are *way above average.*

Guests often tell me that the only reason they cruise is so they can eat as much food as humanly possible in seven days. I've never understood this. Sure, cruise ship food is great—and it's fun to overindulge one week out of the year—but the *only* reason to go on a cruise? When you cruise you have to pay for airfare, ground transportation, boarding passes, port charges, taxes, gratuities, shore excursions, drinks, souvenirs—and sometimes bail, hush money and property damages. But a trip to Golden Coral costs $8.95. You can park your big butt at your favorite table every day of the week and put those suckers out of business.

But, OK, if you're going on a cruise, then yes, be prepared to eat. But make sure you also prepare yourself for the full formal dining room experience. Most ships have one or more formal dining rooms and each guest is scheduled for one of two or three dinner seating times. The most common dining times are 6 p.m., called the "early seating," and 8:15 p.m., called the "late seating." And, in case you've never eaten in a fancy restaurant before, you might want to learn some basic table manners before going on your cruise. Because, although you're free to eat as many of your meals as you want in the buffet restaurant on Lido Deck, if you plan to dine in the main dining room or one of the alternative dining venues such as the gourmet steakhouse or sushi bar, you'll be expected to dress nicely, sit up straight and keep your elbows off the table. But don't feel pressured to say grace before each meal. If you observe other families with their heads bowed in prayer before digging in, don't worry—they're just looking down at their phones.

The formal dining room has dress codes that are usually strictly enforced. On formal night, men will be expected to wear a suit and tie but can get away with a nice collared shirt and a pair of dress pants. And even though most other nights are usually "dress casual" or "casual," don't plan to eat dinner in jean shorts and flip-flops, because the ship's Maître D' is the only person on the ship authorized to bitch slap you for dressing like a douche bag for dinner, and this is a perk he rarely passes up.

Another thing you need to know about dinner in the main dining room is it's going to take a while. Most meals are about seven courses and, with the overwhelming amount of tables your waiter and his team will have to serve, it'll take all seven days of your cruise to complete your meal.

Your dining room waiter and his team of assistant waiters will no doubt be some of the nicest and hardest working people on the ship. Night after night, they'll serve starters, main courses and dessert to sometimes 10 tables or more for almost two hours—twice a night—and yet will always be super attentive and personable. Not only will your waiters answer every question with a smile and get to know you by name, they won't flinch when you order enough food off the menu to make "Mike and Molly" choke. Every night, the dining room menu will feature starters such as crab cakes, shrimp cocktail, French onion soup, and lobster bisque. For your entrée, there'll be steak and lobster, grilled swordfish, meatloaf, herbed chicken, and a variety of pasta dishes. For dessert, you'll choose from tiramisu, crème brullée, baked Alaska, and an assortment of cakes, pies and ice creams. And the best thing is you can have as much as you want. The formal dining room on a cruise ship is the only place in the world where you can order dinner like this: *OK, to start, I'll have two shrimp cocktails, two crab cakes, and a bowl of lobster bisque. Then, for my entrée, I'll have two surf and turfs, two grilled pork chops, two loaded baked potatoes, and a double order of linguine with clam sauce. For dessert, I'll take the apple cobbler, the cherry pie, a bowl of custard, and a fruit plate—because I'm on a diet—and, oh, yeah—a Coke Zero to drink* and

75

have the waiter respond like this: "Come on, Karen Carpenter, you can do better than that!"

Singing for Your Supper

Another thing to look forward to on your cruise is the time during dinner, usually right before dessert is served, when the dining room waiters put down their trays and dance and sing for you as a group. Because, nothing helps you digest your food like watching tired and overworked Filipinos who haven't had a break since lunchtime being humiliated by pretending to know all the words and moves to "Gangham Style."

And, if you're celebrating a birthday or anniversary, please let the Maître D' know so he can come over and sing to you personally. It's his job to make your birthday special by making everyone at the tables surrounding yours hate you for the rest of your cruise.

Chapter 15: The Cruise Director

The ship's cruise director is, more often than not, both the head of the Entertainment Department and the face of the ship. The cruise director is responsible for scheduling and promoting all shipboard shows and activities. The cruise director reports to either the entertainment director or the hotel director, has an assistant cruise director and is supported by a team of Entertainment Department staff members who all want the cruise director's pay and deluxe cabin without any of the work or responsibilities.

But even though the cruise director is in charge of all the on-board entertainment, feel free to complain to him or her about other aspects of your cruise. Don't like the way your steak was cooked in the dining room? Tell the cruise director. The air conditioning in your cabin doesn't work? Tell the cruise director. Your cab driver in the Bahamas overcharged you? Tell the cruise director. Preferably, while she's giving a talk or hosting an activity. Why bring up non-Entertainment-Department issues with Guest Services when you can interrupt the cruise director while she's trying to be entertaining? Just because the cruise director works 100 hours per cruise, is responsible for the behavior, performance and welfare of over 30 department members and spends dozens of hours each week fielding complaints about the quality of shows and activities doesn't mean she doesn't have time to listen to you go on and on about how the lemonade on Lido Deck is too watery. By complaining to the cruise director about little things, you'll show her that you're not merely a clueless guest trying to have a good time on vacation. No, you're a peerless cruising expert possessing superior knowledge and experience of *her* ship, upon which you're sailing *for the very first time*. This will make the cruise director want to hang out with you and your family all cruise long, so don't let the fact that she always has an excuse ready when you ask her to join you for a coffee so you can share your brilliant observations on cruising give you the wrong idea.

The cruise director's responsibilities may include:

Cruise Director's Show

The first time you'll see the cruise director onstage is during the "Welcome aboard Show." Although this show may be called different things on different cruise lines, it's essentially an introductory show filled with music, singing, dancing and comedy that serves as a forum for the cruise director to inform guests about what the ship has to offer. Some cruise directors sing. Some tell jokes. Some interact with the audience. But whatever the cruise director does onstage, it'll put you in the mood to see the rest of the entertainment on board. Because, after watching the cruise director sing, dance and tell jokes for 45 minutes, you'll be praying for the *professional* singers, *professional* dancers, and—for the love of God—the *professional* comedians.

Cruise Director's Talks

During the daytime, on sea days, the cruise director will give various talks intended to both keep guests informed and to help generate revenue. The two main talks are the shore excursion talk and the debarkation talk. The shore excursion talk provides highlights of the various shore excursions, how and when to exit the ship in port, how to maximize your time in port, and how to prevent any mishaps, such as missing the ship. This is a good talk to miss because:

- If you know which shore excursions feature the most amount of walking around in the heat, you'll be prepared with sunscreen, plenty of water and comfortable shoes. This'll rob you of the right to complain about being sunburned, dehydrated and returning to the ship with a limp.
- If you listen to the cruise director describe the best time to get off the ship in the morning, you'll avoid a long wait in line on the gangway. This'll rob you of the ability to complain about wasting 45 minutes of your life you could have spent eating your weight in waffles.

- If you heed the cruise director's warning not to rent scooters or Jet Skis, it will rob you of the ability to sue the cruise line with a clear conscious when you permanently injure yourself while renting a scooter or a Jet Ski.

There's no better feeling than being surprised by something you didn't know during a cruise, losing your temper, and crying, "Nobody told me!" Exiting the ship on your last day is your last opportunity to pull this one. Disembarking the ship can be so time-consuming and confusing that the cruise director will dedicate an entire half-hour talk to this on the last sea day of the cruise.

Don't go.

You wouldn't want to ruin your cruise by being in a good mood on the morning of your departure, would you? You'll want to be able to complain that nobody told you that you had to have your luggage out in the hallway the night before, complain that nobody told you that you couldn't wait in the lobby, and that nobody told you to pack any clothes and toiletries you would need on the morning of your departure so that you won't have to leave the ship naked and afraid. If everyone goes to the debark talk then everyone will know what to do and where to go; therefore, everyone will get off the ship that much more quickly and smoothly, which means you will be forced to relax, smile, and comment to the cruise director, as he says goodbye at the door, how organized and efficient his ship is—and what fun is *that*?

Cruise Director's Announcements

Although the cruise director is known as the face of the ship, she can be better described as the voice of the ship. Several times a day, you'll be treated to the cruise director's chirpy and animated voice as she tries to get you all excited about lame activities such as Bingo, trivia, bean bag tournaments and "pool games." What's more relaxing than waking up unexpectedly at 7 a.m. to hear someone with a cheery English or Australian accent remind you that towel folding class starts at 8 a.m.? Makes you want to jump out of bed, roll up a towel rifle and go towel animal hunting.

Chapter 16: Your Fellow Guests

Although *Cruise Critic* reviews can tell you which ships offer the biggest bang for your buck, one thing they can't tell you is what your fellow passengers will be like on any given cruise. Pick the wrong sailing date, with the wrong guest demographic, and your vacation can go from Cape Canaveral to "Cape Fear" faster than you can say, "Here comes Honey Boo-Boo!"

Even if you book the most poorly reviewed ship in the fleet, the biggest negative surprise of your cruise will be what troublemakers some of your fellow cruisers can be. Those tan lines above their feet? That's where the house arrest ankle bracelets used to be.

Although TV commercials always make cruising look like a care-free adventure, take it from your old pal Jeff the Fun Dude:

- No matter how luxurious your cabin may be, you won't get any rest if your quarrelsome neighbors sound like they're auditioning for "The Jerry Springer Show" on their balcony every night.
- No matter how incredible the food and service in the dining room may be, you're not going to enjoy dinner if the family next to you lets their sugar-addled rug rats run around the table, screeching their heads off as if they were starring in a telethon for Planned Parenthood.
- No matter how efficient and understanding the personnel at Guest Services may be, you'll never get to the front of the line if all 20 members of the same Idiots Anonymous chapter are regaling them with the enthralling narrative of how they mistook the mini safes in their cabins for microwave ovens.
- No matter how funny the comedian in the ship's comedy club may be, you can't enjoy the show if the trailer-park CPAs behind you are fighting over the check, trying to figure out who the hell ordered a drink called "gratuity."

Sure, everyone has to put up with naughty neighbors at home or work alongside first-class boneheads in the office; you expect that. What you don't expect is to pay thousands of dollars to embark upon the vacation of a lifetime only to have it ruined by a handful of inconsiderate knuckleheads whose foster parents never taught them how to behave in public. Expect loud drunks to swear repeatedly in front of your children. Expect giggling morons to drop ice on you from the upper decks. Expect thoughtless jerks to light up cigars in the hot tub. Expect complete idiots to leave their empty coffee mugs in the middle of the stairs so your mother-in-law can fall and break her hip. Expect selfish pigs to swipe the last four slices of banana cream pie from the buffet without asking if you or one of your kids would like one. (OK, expect *me* to do that, too.)

Bottom line: If you think you're getting away from the real world by going on a cruise, you're wrong. Thanks to an abundance of affordable fares on the Internet, the same blockheads who make your life miserable on land are going to follow you up the gangway, dragging their knuckles behind them. They'll cut in line in front of you at the buffet, chat loudly during production shows, and save deck chairs for friends who are never showing up—all the while being totally oblivious to how uncomfortable they're making you feel or how badly they're intimidating your children. And that's just the relatives you'll be cruising with. Complete strangers will be even worse.

These days, cruise lines are doing whatever they can to fill every ship to capacity. The more empty cabins they have, the more money they lose, and the harder it will be for them to keep their prices down. Unfortunately, reduced fares and on-board credit incentives mean that more and more rednecks who've had their RVs repossessed are trading camping for cruising, which means there'll be more people to heatedly debate the verisimilitude of Pro Wrestling right behind you while you're trying to enjoy a romantic sunset with your special someone or, if you're a loser like me, your special smart phone.

Fortunately, the majority of the people you'll meet on your cruise will be friendly, helpful and entertaining. You might even make a few new friends for life. In fact, the number of nice people you'll meet will allow you to suffer the fools more gladly and, more than likely, encourage you to book another cruise right away. Of course, as you're standing in line to meet with the ship's on-board future cruise expert, some idiot will cut in line right in front of you.

But, as for the imbeciles, nitwits and pinheads? Remember, it's not a crime to push somebody overboard if nobody sees you do it. Besides, that won't be the first time somebody's "gotten away with murder" while cruising.

Part 4: Enjoying Your Cruise

Chapter 17: Activities

Every cruise ship has a team of Entertainment Department staff members whose backgrounds in acting, dance, public relations, stand-up comedy or musical theater have prepared them for careers in the Entertainment Industry, making them uniquely qualified to host "fun and exciting" cruise-ship activities even a monkey could host. Unfortunately, monkeys aren't allowed on cruise ships. So make sure you attend as many shipboard activities as possible and watch your hard-working and dedicated Entertainment staff members practice the lost art of the forced smile. (Because they often where similar uniforms, here's how you can tell the difference between an Entertainment staff member and a Kids' Club staff member: one deals with a bunch of whining, immature babies, while the other deals with their children.) Here are some tips for getting the most out of the most common on-board activities:

Bingo

- Do *not* ask how big the jackpots will be before buying your Bingo cards. It's important that you buy a lot of cards without bothering to ask anyone how much money you'll actually have the chance of winning. That way, after realizing you've spent $60 to win $300, you can lose your temper, complain about how cheap the cruise line is, and ultimately confuse the 23-year-old woman handing you your prize, because that $300 equals her paycheck for a 90-hour work week.
- Buy more Bingo cards than you can handle at once. Since it's the job of the kid calling the games to make the proceedings as entertaining as possible by throwing out little jokes here and there ("The next ball is B-8. As in, 'Try not to fall overboard because there are lots of sharks in the water and you will 'B-8'."), it's your job to totally ignore the jokes and

keep shouting, "Slow down!" Playing more cards than you can handle allows you to do three things at once:

- o 1) Get angry during what is supposed to be a fun and lighthearted activity.
- o 2) Spoil the mood for everybody else.
- o 3) Embarrass the kid onstage who is simply trying to get both this game and this contract over with so he can pay off his student loans, get on with his life, and hopefully wind up in some kind of career that'll offer him enough financial security in middle age so that he'll never have to pin all his hopes and dreams for a comfortable retirement on being the kind of jackass who ruins other people's fun during a stupid game of Bingo.

Trivia

So what if you don't know the answers to the trivia questions the host asks? That doesn't mean you shouldn't win a prize, right? This whole business of the prize, usually a toy trophy shaped like a cruise ship, going to the one person who answers more questions than everyone else is a load of crap. What makes that person so special that he gets a prize and you don't? Just because that person knows all the answers to the trivia questions asked during a trivia game doesn't mean you should lose. Let the host know how unfair this is. Upbraid, browbeat and dress down the host for being biased towards the winner. Let the kid know that you've written down her name and are prepared to write a letter to the cruise line telling them how much she ruined your cruise by embarrassing you in front of your fellow guests by denying you the prize you're *entitled* to simply because you *want* it.

Beanbag Toss Tournaments

Beanbag tossing or "cornhole," as it's known in the Midwest, is not some silly game wherein senior citizens in brown sandals and black socks kill an hour or two on a sunny day, making new friends and getting a little fresh air; this is serious business, best conducted after drinking an entire bucket of cold beer in the tropical heat. Shout, scream and swear if children are on your team, because it's about time the kiddies learned the harsh reality of the brave new world of Lido Deck recreational activities. Most important, make sure you commit 100 percent to annihilating the other team and proving to them that they're pathetic losers who have no business being on a cruise ship. It'll make you feel that much better about yourself the next day when you're on a tour bus observing the poverty, squalor and misery that make up the harsh reality of life on a small Caribbean island.

Karaoke

When I first came to work for my cruise line after a long and successful career as a nationally touring comedian, they asked me if I would be interested in becoming a karaoke host so I could use humor to make karaoke more enjoyable. I said, "If you want to make karaoke more enjoyable, don't have it." I'm not saying that I hate karaoke; I'm just saying that if I want to listen to some drunken idiot butcher Billy Joel songs all night, I'll go to a Billy Joel concert.

But it's OK if *you* like karaoke. Different strokes for different folks, right? Just be sure to show up to the karaoke lounge a full hour before karaoke starts. This will give you the right to sing more songs than the hundreds of people who arrive at the advertised starting time. By camping out early, you're sending a message to the Universe that karaoke is the only thing that gives you joy in life and that you're a dedicated karaoke professional. This is *not* merely a fun activity during which any passenger who paid for the cruise can hang out and sing a song or two; this is a *concert* and *you* are the *star*. And because you were there before the host even set up the karaoke machine, you get to sing every other song over the entire three-hour karaoke session. If, for some reason, the host doesn't fully appreciate your star power, and perhaps even has the audacity to allow other guests to sing a song, make sure you scream at her in front of all the other guests and threaten to have her fired.

This is show business, damn it—you didn't come on this cruise to be on vacation; you came on this cruise to share your talent as a middle-aged white male who sings deliciously off-key renditions of Adele tunes.

Men's Hairy Chest Competition

If you decide to cruise on a Carnival ship, for example, one of the things you might see—or be forced to see if you just so happen to be up on Lido Deck trying to relax and mind your own business—is the men's hairy chest competition. This is an activity for folks for whom "The Maury Show" is too high-brow. The entertainment host starts things off by walking around the open deck, looking for very hairy men. The men then dance around onstage to the hoots and hollers of inebriated passengers. Every time you witness this spectacle you can expect the same cast of characters:

- **The hot guy.** This is a good-looking hunk with a "Magic Mike" body but absolutely no body hair whatsoever. This guy gets the party started and gets the ladies screaming and clapping. Obviously, his guy never wins, because he's in great shape and has no hair and so the host does not want to insult the out-of-shape hairy guys who actually think that winning this thing will be some kind of achievement.
- **The fat guy.** This Chris Farley wannabe has only one move: rubbing his hands over his stomach while making lewd gestures with his tongue. This Cheetos-loving Chippendale never fails to get the guys in the audience clapping and whooping it up, if only because they're so glad they're not him. (Even though most of them *are.*)
- **The old guy.** This gentleman, usually in his 70s or 80s, has lots of unruly grey hair, looks like some kind of second-tier Dr. Seuss character and is always wearing some kind of goofy hat, shorts or novelty sunglasses. Not sexy. Not funny.

Just pathetic. And sad. *Very* sad. Because, this is the dude who almost always wins.

The only reason this idiotic activity is still on cruise ships is because folks still go crazy for it. If you really want to have some fun, the first time you see the hairy chest competition, just stand there with your arms folded and shout, "You're all a bunch of idiots! How did mouth-breathing morons like you ever save up enough money to go on a cruise in the first place—how many trips to your local Coinstar machine did you have to make?!" This will get you a free drink. (But only if you're on *my* ship and I happen to hear you before a bunch of horny old ladies start beating you to death with their walkers.)

Miniature Golf

Staying with the theme of spending thousands of dollars to go on a cruise so you can take part in activities that you can play for a few bucks on land, right down the street from your home, most ships feature a miniature golf course. In case you've never played mini golf before, here's a tip for tearing up the Astro Turf: If you have small children who can barely walk, let alone hold a golf club, make sure you play their round during the busiest time of the day. And don't start playing until you can get in front of a large group of adults who take mini golf seriously. They'll get a big kick out of watching your little munchkins take 10,000 swings just to hit the ball once and then waddle over, pick it up and throw it three holes over. If you want to make the experience even more enjoyable for your fellow cruisers, be sure to yell at your kids as they roll around on the course making happy-happy noises; because, the only thing more fun than watching a 3-year-old turn a 30-minute game of putt-putt into an all-day affair is to watch him being punished by a parent too stupid to know that toddlers are too young for mini golf.

Scavenger Hunts

The important thing to remember when participating in any shipboard activity is that you're usually playing for some cheap prize, such as a plastic trophy or medallion. So you better take the scavenger hunt seriously. This prize may not mean a lot to you, but if there are children on your team, well, they probably won't care, either; but, if there are other adults on your team, winning the prize will surely mean a lot to them. So when they decide to cheat, just play along as if your life depends on it—because it *does*.

The best thing about being on a scavenger hunt on a ship you're still unfamiliar with is it gives you a chance to interact with hardworking crew members. Anytime you're confused as to where the clue on your scavenger hunt is sending you—or you simply can't find the item you're looking for after several tries—seek out anyone wearing a nametag. Well, OK, not just *anyone* with a nametag. You'll want to ask someone wearing a nametag who is obviously extremely busy cleaning something, repairing something, or helping other guests. No need to get the crew member's attention, wait for him to finish what he's doing, or even introduce yourself. Just shout, "Hey, you—where can I get a towel animal, a bar of soap and a tube sock?! I need them now! Now! NOW!" Oh, and make sure you pick crew members who are extremely shy and have a hard time with English. That way, they'll just smile, nod their heads and laugh nervously. If you pick a crew member with a strong command of the English language, however, he'll say, "Have you tried looking in your cabin, Jackass?!"

Chapter 18: Shore Excursions

Although there's a lot to do when your ship's at sea, new and wondrous adventures await you ashore. But have the urge to remain on the ship and eat yourself into a coma while everyone else is wasting time in port? Snap out of it, Gilligan! You're not (just) some fat and lazy American on vacation; you're an intrepid explorer in search of danger and excitement—so slather on that sunblock, suck up that gut and whip out that American Express card; because, a daring adventurer such as yourself is going to want to splurge on some shore excursions for you and your family so you can actually go out and *experience*—not just visit—the ports. Unless, of course, your idea of a good time is wandering aimlessly around a port area that is the mother of all tourist traps, screaming, "No! No! No! Yes! No! Yes! Hell no! Hell yes!" to locals trying to sell you fake jewelry, cheap T-shirts, imitation leather goods, marijuana, wood carvings, prostitutes, wool blankets in summertime, and Mexican wrestling masks.

So, in order to help you maximize your fun in the sun, here are five of the most popular shore excursions for you to choose from:

Excursion # 1: Swimming with the dolphins. Millions of Americans are sailing to the Caribbean this year for the warm sunshine, enchanting evening breezes, sapphire waters, and the chance to swim with cute and cuddly dolphins that weigh 1,100 pounds and can crush a small child like a warm Junior Mint. But despite what the critics might say, swim-with-the-dolphins programs are a great opportunity for dolphins, the second-most intelligent creatures on the planet, to bond with tourists, the *least* intelligent creatures on the planet.

Not only have dolphin encounter excursions become increasingly popular in the Caribbean in the past decade, but the dolphins dig them, too. A former dolphin trainer, who spoke candidly with me on the condition that I twist his words around, told me that dolphins love being in captivity, where they can perform the same boring tricks over and over again with overweight tourists and their snot-nosed offspring holding onto their fins as they bang their sensitive snouts on the walls of their claustrophobic pens instead of swimming free in the deep blue ocean, where the only tourists they'll meet are drunken cruisers who fall overboard.

"Dolphins are beautiful and amazing creatures in their natural habitat," the trainer told me. "But stick them in a cage and they become sad, frustrated and aggressive, making it that much easier for them to relate to humans."

Excursion # 2: Snorkeling and scuba diving. Snorkeling is a particularly popular activity among junior cruisers because kids are less apt to be unpleasantly surprised at how nut-shrinking cold the water in the Caribbean can be, less apt to become disappointed or angry when unusually strong currents make it difficult to observe underwater life, and less apt to get upset when their eyes are awash with stinging salt water because their parents were too tipsy from complimentary tequila to properly adjust their masks for them.

The primary appeal of snorkeling for parents is that it doesn't require the expense, equipment and training needed for scuba diving. But if honest-to-goodness scuba diving is more your thing, then you'll have to get certified first if you want to dive on your own. If you're not certified, then you'll have to either dive with a guide or get hired as an uncertified guide for other non-certified tourists.

Shore excursion # 3: Zip-lining. Are you overweight, out of shape and afraid of heights? Then this is the perfect excursion for you. If you don't have fun, then your bored guides certainly will because they can definitely use a good laugh.

Shore excursion # 4: Parasailing. Each year, an estimated three to five million people participate in parasailing. This popular activity is one of the most exciting things you can do in port because it's largely unregulated and known for serious accidents frequently caused by faulty equipment. There are: no federal regulations or guidelines that establish specific training or certification for parasailing operators; no requirement for inspection of the parasailing equipment; and no requirement to shut down operations during nasty weather conditions. For these reasons alone, serious thrill seekers are sure to get their money's worth.

If you're still not sold on the idea of being suspended 500 feet above the ocean's surface, where simple things such as a weak towline, strong winds, or a worn harness can cause a tragic accident, then perhaps the fact that there are no rules or laws preventing you from buying a half-priced bottle of rum at the duty-free shop and drinking it during your flight might seal the deal.

Shore excursion # 5: Jet Skis and ATVs. Can't decide between renting a Jet Ski or a four-wheeler? Then get a package deal so you can do both in one day. That way, you can break your neck *and* your back. So don't just lounge around Lido Deck nursing your strawberry daiquiri; book a shore excursion today. There'll be plenty of time for lounging when you're in traction in the ICU.

Chapter 19: Live Entertainment

Production Shows

If you're a fan of live entertainment, you might want to do a little online research before choosing which ship to go on. Every cruise line is known for featuring different types of entertainment and each ship in that line usually has a different lineup of production shows that can vary greatly in quality. Royal Caribbean, for example, is known for their elaborate ice dancing shows presented on their indoor ice-skating rinks. Norwegian is known for showing Ingmar Bergman films and then paying $100,000 to any American passenger who points out that Bergman was Swedish, not Norwegian (so far, no takers). Carnival, known for having some of the best production shows on the Seven Seas, has been rolling out new shows from a production company called Playlist Productions. These audiovisual extravaganzas take popular tunes you've been listening to your entire life and bring them to the stage in the form of full-blown musical productions featuring professional singers and dancers rocking the house. The female singers and dancers in these shows usually wear skimpy, sexy costumes that feature a lot of leg, so, if you're a wife and mother, you'll get an awesome aerobic workout during these shows by constantly putting your hands over your pubescent boys' eyes, in between slapping your husband into another time zone.

Lounge Bands

If you enjoy listening to or dancing to live music, your cruise will no doubt have just what the doctor ordered. There'll be a soloist, duo or band in every area of the ship. In the atrium. On the Lido Deck. In the brew pub. Hell, pull open your shower curtain and you'll find a Ukrainian with a ukulele, ready to serenade you with Jimmy Buffet songs. My point is there'll be a lot of great musicians on your cruise and none of their set lists will overlap; because, although they rarely have a chance to watch each other perform, they do have plenty of time to compare notes since they all share the same cabin.

Most ships have a very talented band that takes up residence in one of the mid or aft lounges, just about every night of the cruise. The lounge band is responsible for breathing life and atmosphere into the lounge with a diverse playlist that caters to a wide range of musical tastes and that keeps cruise-ship passengers of all ages tapping their toes and shaking their booties. Besides, where else are you going to see a Filipino sing Journey songs without having to pay to see Journey?

Variety Shows

If full-blown production shows don't float your boat, you ship will probably have a variety act scheduled in the main theater on one or more nights. Usually featuring a magician, juggler or hypnotist, these shows are called "variety" shows because they feature different acts trotting out the same lame cruise-ship entertainment tropes in a *variety* of ways. The hypnotist will make some out-of-shape dude dance around the stage like "Magic Mike." The magician will do one or two tricks that "didn't work" and then make a joke along the lines of "How much did you folks pay for this show?" and then bring a small child onstage to assist in the trick, getting big laughs by talking to the child as one would to an adult and, of course, getting even more big laughs at the child's expense. The juggler will no doubt do some kind of trick involving machetes and a volunteer from the audience and then act as if there's a good chance the volunteer will be maimed or killed during the stunt. But, much to your chagrin, everything will turn out just fine.

Stand-up Comedy

Because I've spent the past several years managing my cruise line's first-ever full-time comedy club on one of their ships, I feel uniquely qualified to offer you tips for getting the most yucks for your cruising bucks. In order to fully appreciate a stand-up comedy show on a cruise ship, you'll need to keep in mind that your fellow guests are there to see *you,* not the comedian onstage. So make sure you sit in the front row and heckle. Even though this might be your first cruise and your first time seeing a live comedy show, the show could not go on without *you.* Remember that *you* are the center of the comedy universe and your ship's comedian was not booked for his engagement until it was confirmed that *you,* too, would be on the ship. Don't let the fact that they have comedy on the ship every single cruise throw you; the show would *not* be possible without *you* distracting the comedian and making him come up with funny put-down lines on the spot. It's almost impossible for a comedian to hone a 30-minute show after only writing and performing every day for 10 years without your help during *one* of the *thousands* of shows he has performed, so make sure you sit up front, drink as many Long Island Iced Teas as possible, and talk your head off with no regard whatsoever for either the performer onstage or your fellow guests seated around you.

More important, if the comedian tells a joke that offends *you,* make sure you let everybody know. Just because a comedian is a fully grown adult who makes his living delivering his opinions in a humorous way doesn't mean it's *his* opinion that counts. Just because the lights are pointed at *him* and he's speaking into a microphone and you're *not* doesn't mean it's *his* show. It's *your* show. Stand-up is not about the *comedian's* opinions. It's not even about your fellow guests' opinions. It's all about *your* opinions, baby. Of course, this could be a little confusing for the cruise line because they hired the comedian and put *his* photo on the marquee. Your name isn't even listed in the daily entertainment schedule. But don't let that stop you. Anytime the comedian is making fun of things that might upset other people but not you, laugh your head off. If you're skinny and he makes fun of fat people, laugh. If you're a brunette and he makes fun of blondes, laugh. If you're Republican and he makes fun of Democrats, laugh. But the moment the comedian makes fun of something that hits close to home with you—the skinny brunette Republican, nobody else in that showroom has the right to laugh. So as soon as you hear

96

something that offends *you*, storm out of the room and race straight down to Guest Services to complain. But be sure to plug your fingers in your ears as you're fleeing the club, feeling all indignant and full of yourself, so you don't have to listen to the sound of *500 other people laughing.*

The Guest Talent Show

Another popular option exercised by many cruise lines is to schedule a guest talent show that enables both talented and not-so-talented guests to feel like superstars for an evening while saving the cruise lines big money by not having to hire real entertainers. If you're lucky, you'll be treated to dance or musical numbers by guests who are either full-time or part-time entertainers at home or perhaps folks who do Community Theater, play in bar bands, church ensembles, or in the classic rock group Foghat. But that's not what the majority of guests come to see when they come to the guest talent show. Although some guests will be going specifically to watch their friends or family members perform, the majority of guests come looking for a train wreck: the tone-deaf housewife butchering Adele's "Hello" or the drunken grandpa playing "Stairway to Heaven" on an accordion.

The Piano Bar

The ship's piano bar is the perfect place to hang out if you're an aforementioned drunken idiot who loves shouting "woo!" for no reason whatsoever. If you think that it's a totally original and novel move to sway your hands in the air singing along to "Sweet Caroline" and aren't the least bit embarrassed by people deciding not to go into a room because of the behavior you're exhibiting, then the piano bar is for you. If you're too @#$-ing shallow and immature to simply sit the @#$% down, shut the @#$% up, and listen to an extremely talented piano player enjoy his time in the spotlight without your needing to scream and shout or fall down on the floor laughing like an idiot, then you are exactly the type of redneck the cruise line was thinking of when they decided to put a piano bar on the ship. So go, get drunk, sing along, make an ass out of yourself, and send as many other guests heading for the door as possible. That's what the piano bar is there for, so enjoy.

Chapter 20: Ports of Call

Taxis

Traveling by taxi in a Caribbean port is a little different than back in the States. If you need a cab in New York City, for example, you might as well try to get a commercial jetliner to land on 5th Avenue and wave you aboard. If the cabbie ignores your shouts, whistles and dramatic gestures, you can always lie down in the street and see if he stops. (I wouldn't bet on it.)

Nothing in North America prepares you for the aggressiveness of the cabbies in the Caribbean. They'll follow you down the street, doing cartwheels, juggling machetes and shouting, "Taxi! Taxi! Taxi!" Apparently, they didn't get the word that most Americans are so lazy they'd take a cab from their kitchen to their bedroom if one were available. They simply don't realize that you don't need to hard sell a taxi to someone who would push an old lady to the ground to steal one.

Restaurants

Although you can certainly go back to the ship for a free lunch, one of the fun things about being on a cruise is exploring the ports and finding restaurants you wouldn't normally eat at. For example, if you're a McDonald's person, one of the most common ports, the island of St. Maarten, has a KFC. But unlike in the States, the chicken at a KFC on St. Maarten is fresh. In fact, they'll usually let you go outside and pick your own chicken from the ones running around the parking lot.

The great thing about going to American fast food franchises in the Caribbean is it'll make you appreciate the lousy service in America that much more. If you think the kids at your local Subway are slow and unfriendly, try ordering a foot-long sub on the island of St. Thomas. If you're lucky, the kid will have your sandwich ready by the time you return to the island on your next cruise.

Beaches

When going to the beach in port, you'll have two choices: public beach or private. You can find the best public beaches with a little simple online research or you can ask your taxi driver. But keep in mind that your cabbie will usually pick a beach where one of his relatives owns a souvenir shop, bar or restaurant. It's hard to find secluded beaches in the Caribbean because everyone wants you to go to the tourist traps where everyone's homies will be trying to sell you a massage, trinkets, or lunch in their restaurant. (Ain't *that* a *beach?*)

A popular option for private beaches is to buy an all-day pass to an all-inclusive beach resort. For one price, usually anywhere from $50 to $100 per person and usually offered as a shore excursion on your ship, you can swim, eat, drink and sun bathe. Basically, everything you already paid to do on the ship.

Shopping

If shopping is your thing, here are seven tips for shopping in port:

1. **Haggle. Haggle. Haggle.** You'd be surprised at how many prices are negotiable. Mainly because a fair amount of the merchandise will be either fake or stolen. If you see an item you like that costs $50, don't be afraid to offer $35 or $40 for it, because that's still $35 or $40 more than the vendor paid for it.
2. **No debit or credit cards.** It's always best to rely on cash when shopping in port. Avoid using debit and credit cards unless you want to spend the first few weeks after your cruise disputing fraudulent charges with a Customer Service representative who is talking to you from a call center in Mumbai, India, yet somehow expects you to believe that "Scott" is his real name.
3. **Don't be afraid to shop at stores other than the ones "recommended" by the cruise line.** You can often find

better deals at other stores since they're not paying commissions to the cruise lines and have less overhead. Besides, the rush you'll get from visiting shops hidden down winding side streets without getting mugged will be more than worth it.

4. **Stay away from the cheap T-shirts.** As tempting as it may be, don't waste your money on the "3 for $10" T-shirt deals. The quality of these shirts is extremely poor and they usually shrink several sizes after just one washing. The only reason you should ever buy shirts of such low quality is if they're souvenirs for your friends and loved ones back home. They're never going to wear them anyway.

5. **Have larger items shipped to you.** Instead of bringing larger items back on the ship and then having to carry them off with you on disembarkation day, you can ask many of the in-port shops to ship your purchases home for you. But ask the store about their shipping policies before purchasing large items. A common scam is to sell you a box 10 or 20 times bigger than needed so they can smuggle some friends or relatives into the States with your coconut-shell cuckoo clock or whatever-the-hell-else else you bought after having one too many banana daiquiris. And make sure you get their email and phone number because you'll probably want to contact the store every few months while you wait for your merchandise to arrive.

6. **No ganja, mon!** No matter how old you are, what you look like or how you dress, the locals will try to sell you pot. Don't fall for it. Because, if they can't tell pot smokers from nonsmokers, what are the odds they can tell good weed from bad?

7. **Stay in the tourist areas.** You're an American alone on a Caribbean Island, so no wandering off the beaten path— or you might get beaten. If the idea of not being able to go wherever you want safely bothers you, then forget

the cruise and go someplace safe like Ferguson, Missouri.

Duty-free Stores

For some reason, most cruise ship passengers simply cannot wrap their heads around the concept of duty-free shopping. After they buy their liquor, cigarettes or what have you, they start freaking out: "What if I'm over my allowance—what if I have to pay a duty—oh my God—do you think I'll get arrested? Will I have to post bail?" Duty-free stores make a killing by making tourists think they're getting away with something: "Come on, let's overpay for everything in the store because there's NO DUTY!"

Let me simplify things for you: "duty" is simply a fancy word for "tax." So if an item is duty-free it means you don't have to pay tax on it. If you go over your allowance, which is around 40 cents per person (don't quote me on that), then you have to pay sales tax—or *"duty"*—on the remaining balance, which is no big deal. But be careful. A lot of duty-free stores like to trick you. They bet on your not knowing that "duty" simply means "sales tax," so they'll overcharge you big time for small items such as candy and toiletries. You're so happy you're not paying "duty" that you don't even notice that you're paying $12 for a Kit-Kat Bar simply because it's in a special gift box shaped like a parrot.

Missing the Ship

If you're concerned about missing your ship because of a delayed flight, don't be. Missing your ship in her homeport is not that big of a deal. All you'll have to do is shell out a couple thousand bucks for a last-minute flight to your ship's first port, spend the night or two in an overpriced hotel room, and then catch an overpriced taxi to the port the day your ship arrives. Should the language barrier between you and your cabbie cause you to miss the ship again, just repeat the entire process until suicidal.

Now, missing the ship during your cruise because you return from port too late—that's a different matter. If you miss the ship in this case, you'll have nobody but yourself to blame. Thankfully, there are preventative measures you can take in order to avoid being left behind:

1. **Know what time your ship is departing.** This is easier said than done. Because, in order to hear the multiple announcements the cruise director will make each time you arrive in a new port, you'll have to take your earbuds out of your ears. So, if you don't hear the announcements telling you what time "back on board" is, you can always check your ship's daily schedule, but then that would require you to stop looking at your smartphone for five seconds. Fortunately, you can always ask the crew at the gangway, but then you would have to stop shoving food in your mouth long enough to talk.

2. **Allow extra time for getting back to the ship.** Ship happens: cabs get stuck in traffic, buses break down, and lines form in shops that make checking out longer than you might expect. So if you really want to make sure you don't miss the ship, walk off the gangway, turn around, and then march right back onto the ship.

3. **Book a shore excursion.** Want to tour a part of the island that may be a haul and a half from the port or perhaps is infamous for having brutal traffic jams? Then you might want to think twice about going off on your own. Instead, book one of the cruise line's branded shore excursions. That way, if there are any delays getting back to the ship, the captain will wait for you. Then, instead of thanking the cruise line for waiting for you, you can complain about the tour excursion making you late. In which case you might get a free shore excursion to the nearest hospital, courtesy of the shore excursion manager.

4. **Don't leave the ship without ID.** Being stranded on a Caribbean island is one thing, but being stranded with no identification really sucks. Should you miss the ship and

don't at least have your driver's license, you're not going to be able to get a flight home, which means you'll have to live on the island. But, without an ID, you won't be able to get a job or an apartment, which means you won't be able to find a place to live or support yourself. The good news is you can just wait for the cruise ship to come back the following week and then you can apply to be a waiter or housekeeper.

5. **Keep a credit card on you.** The cruise line is not financially responsible for getting you to the next port if you miss the ship. Your travel to the next port, or back home, is on your dime, as are any necessary hotel bills and meal expenses you accrue in the process. So don't leave the ship without a credit card that has enough available credit it on it to book a plane ticket if necessary. Better yet, don't leave the ship at all.

6. **Carry the ship's daily schedule with you**. The ship's departure time is right there on the front cover. If you can't figure out that the best way to remember what time you're supposed to be back on the ship is to keep a copy of the ship's schedule in your pocket, you're not going to be able to figure out how to get off the island if you miss the ship. So again, *don't leave the ship.*

7. **Create a contingency plan.** If you do miss the ship, go into the cruise terminal and ask the port agents for help. If they're not too busy laughing at you, they might loan you a pair of flippers so you can try to catch up with the ship.

Chapter 21: Hooking Up

First of all, hooking up with crew members can get them fired. So, if you get turned down by a crew member, that means you're not good looking enough to risk being fired. So try your luck with your fellow guests, instead, Ugly.

Singles Events

Going on a cruise just for the chance of hooking up with someone? What is wrong with you? Don't you realize how much more useful all the money you'll spend on a cruise would be at home? If you're a chick, you could get your hair done and go to the spa. If you're a dude, you could buy fashionable new clothes and go on a lot of expensive dates. Hell, for two grand you could hit an Ikea and refurnish your apartment and make it someplace a chick would want to spend the night at.

Yeah, you can get lucky on a cruise. But you can also get lucky at Wal-Mart if you play your coupons right. But although you can meet other poor and desperate singles at Wal-Mart, that's not what you go to Wal-Mart for. And that's not what you should go on a cruise for, either. You go to Wal-Mart to save money on groceries and you go on a cruise to save money on your vacation. So why not stay home, watch some steamy Cinemax movie, and then shop at Whole Foods, instead?

But if you do go on a cruise, the ship will no doubt schedule singles events. Such events will usually be listed in the ship's schedule as "Singles Meet" and will be an un-hosted event. Meaning, it'll be just you and the bartender. (Out of respect for the environment, this joke was recycled from an earlier chapter.)

GLBT Events

Any event listed as "Friends of Dorothy" is usually a get-together for members of the Gay, Lesbian, Bisexual and Transgender community. It does not mean a get-together for fans of the movie *The Wizard of Oz.* By the way, if you're a straight person who thinks getting together to talk about *The Wizard of Oz* while on vacation is a fun activity, perhaps you should rethink your sexual orientation.

The Nightclub

The aforementioned nightclub is one of the most fun hangouts on the ship. Where else can you watch old ladies with walkers twerk to gangsta rap?

My favorite thing to do in the nightclub is to watch middle-aged men hit on 20-something women:

MIDDLE-AGED DUDE:

"Hey, cupcake, can I buy you a drink?"

HOT YOUNG THING:

"Sure."

MIDDLE-AGED DUDE (Thinking to himself):

"Alright—this chick's into older men."

HOT YOUNG THING (Thinking to herself):

"Wow—this geezer just saved me nine bucks."

Another great thing about your ship's nightclub is you get to request which songs you get to dance to. Simply walk up to the DJ booth and start tapping the DJ on the shoulder while he's busy mixing a song, making sure to ignore his hints that he's too busy right now to talk to you. Then, when you finally do have his attention, be sure to request the most overexposed song on the planet. That way, when he tells you that he already played that song three times before you entered the club and will need to wait awhile before spinning it again, you can march right down to Guest

Services and complain. (And while you're down there bending the Guest Services associate's ear, the DJ will happily play your song.)

Part 5: Finishing Your Cruise

Chapter 22: Booking Your Next Cruise

On-board Future Cruise Expert

OK, let's say you're on the last day of your cruise and it hasn't been exactly what you thought it'd be. Your cabin wasn't as nice as you thought it'd be; the food wasn't as tasty as you thought it'd be; the production shows weren't as entertaining as you thought they'd be; the comedians weren't as funny as you thought they'd be; the crew members weren't as friendly as you thought they'd be; the ship wasn't as fancy as you thought it'd be; the ports weren't as pretty as you thought they'd be; your shore excursions weren't as exciting as you thought they'd be. You argued with your travel mates, didn't meet any fun or interesting people, and you left your brand-new digital camera in the back of a cab. In fact, you were so disappointed that you decided to go down to Guest Services and complain, where they surprised you with a free-drink coupon and $25 on-board credit. So now there's only one thing to do: book your next cruise while still on board. For this, you'll want to pay a visit to your ship's on-board future cruise expert, who won't be, of course, as much of an expert as you thought she'd be.

Booking Incentives

Your on-board future cruise expert can help you find the best deal possible on your next cruise, thereby instilling a sense of loyalty in you. You see, even though it's you who are *paying* the cruise line, the cruise line wants *you* to be loyal to *them*. And how do they achieve this? By offering you incentives to cruise with them over and over again. Just like in real life, when you try to get your friends, family and coworkers to be loyal to you by buying them things, doing favors for them, and basically kissing their butts, right? Works beautifully doesn't it?

Of course not.

Be nice to your loved ones and then they'll have an incentive to take you for granted or take advantage of you. So now it's your turn to take advantage of the cruise line. Get as much free crap and as many discounts as you can and then, when the well dries up, jump ship and switch to another cruise line. It's the American way.

Some typical incentives:

- A serious discount for your next cruise—up to as much as 50 percent or half off (whichever is cheaper). Discounts this big are meant to make you feel good by showing you how much you overpaid for your previous cruise.
- On-board credit, sometimes as much as $250— enough to buy a few toiletries in the ship's gift shop.
- You get to pick the exact cabin you want and will be guaranteed that cabin. Of course, you won't actually get that cabin; instead, you'll get some free-drink coupons and—you guessed it—$25 in on-board credit.

Learning from Your Mistakes

Some new cruisers don't have an enjoyable experience because they choose the wrong cruise line for their first cruise. Many others, however, simply don't have an enjoyable experience because they're insufferable dingleberries with lousy personalities and zero common sense. If you're the kind of person who considers being labeled an insufferable dingleberry with a lousy personality and zero common sense a badge of honor, here's how you should behave on your first cruise:

- **Avoid the main dining room because you don't feel like dressing up.** Many first-time cruisers eat at the buffet every night for dinner because they don't feel like putting on pants or shoes. While you're free to never set foot in the main dining room, the cuisine in the dining room is always way more palatable than the grub on Lido Deck. So why bother

109

going on a cruise just to eat from the buffet every night when you can simply stay home, feed your face at Golden Coral, and use the money you'll save to buy yourself some new sweatpants and flip-flops at TJ Maxx?

- **Show up late for dinner**. When you show up late to the dining room, it delays din-din for you and your tablemates. Your waiters prefer to keep the entire table on the same course so that no one will get their main dishes until everyone orders and polishes off their soups, salads and appetizers. So, if you get between your fellow passengers and their entrées, those people are going to spend the whole cruise being pissed at you, and that means you're not going to have as much fun. Part of the fun of a cruise is becoming friends with your tablemates, so if you're not going to watch your mouth, at least watch your watch.
- **Book an early flight home**. All cruise lines recommend booking no flights earlier than noon on disembarkation day if you're flying out of your ship's homeport city. Even if your ship's schedule lists your arrival as 7 a.m., booking a 9 a.m. or earlier flight is a boneheaded move. Sometimes, getting off of the ship is quick and easy. Other times, long lines can make going through Immigration and Customs a nightmare. So book your flight home for the afternoon and avoid a stressful disembarkation process or worrying about missing your plane. Of course, this will rob you of one last thing to complain about before leaving the ship and that could take some of the fun out of debark morning for you.
- **Use your cellphone as if it's a third arm**. Using your cell phone on the ship can cost anywhere from three to six dollars a minute; but, hey—if you can afford a cruise, you can afford a cell phone bill that costs as much as a cruise.
- **Try to do everything the first day**. No need to take time to enjoy your time at sea. You'll have plenty of time to relax back at work, after your vacation.
- **Skip the muster drill**. Why go to the drill and pay attention just because your life and those of your friends and family

could depend on it? Stay by the pool and play on your phone, Jerky.

- **Don't plan for missed ports**. Although your ship's captain will do everything in his power to visit all of your scheduled ports, weather and other circumstances can cause a ship to miss a port stop or two, especially if those ports are tender ports. So go ahead and plan your entire cruise around one particular port so you can bitch and moan when the captain puts your safety above your desire to pound raspberry mojitos while contracting the Zika virus.

- **Bring your own alcohol on the ship**. If you really want to hit it off with the crew, cram as many bottles of booze as you can into your luggage. Because, once Security confiscates your liquor and donates it to the weekly crew party I mentioned earlier, you'll be one of the most popular guests on the ship.

- **Save seats**. If you can save a whole row of seats at your kid's piano recital for your friends and family who are running a little behind, why not on a cruise? Whether at a popular show in the evening or in prime spots on the Lido Deck near the pool, there is nothing wrong with saving a seat or two for someone who is on their way. I mean it's not like the other guests on the cruise paid as much as you did to come on the cruise and might want to use the seats too, right?

Chapter 23: Souvenirs

Shopping for souvenirs is an important part of the cruising experience. Regardless of where you cruise to, buying a small knick-knack for either yourself or for others is essential. But, whether you're seeking the perfect memento that will remind you of your cruise, want to treat a member of your inner circle who couldn't make the cruise, or reward somebody who's watching your house, pets or kids, make sure you wait till the very last minute, because stress and indecision make souvenir shopping that much easier:

YOU:

"Do you think Sandy would like this wood carving of a dolphin? If she ever gets out of jail, finds a job and rents a mobile home, she could put it on her mantle."

SPOUSE:

"Sure, whatever! Just buy the stupid thing and let's get the hell out of here! We're going to miss the ship!"

YOU:

"Well, if you think it's stupid maybe I should get her this ceramic skull or maybe this wool blanket with the Dallas Cowboy's logo, even though her husband is a Steelers fan."

SPOUSE

"No, the wooden dolphin is a priceless work out art—get it, for the love of God, and let's *go!* It'll be worth lots of money someday and so maybe she can unload it on E-Bay and then be able to go on your next cruise with you so I won't have to risk being stuck in Mexico for the rest of my life because you can't make up your mind about some piece-of-crap souvenir! *Pay* for the damn thing and let's *GO!*"

Whom to Buy for?

If you're on a cruise with your family, then you're going to want to get a little something for everybody. If you have young boys and one of your ports is in Mexico, then you're going to want to get them Mexican wrestling masks. They'll wear them at dinner. They'll wear them in the pool. They'll wear them to bed. And, they'll wear them on the trip home—unless you're flying, in which case the TSA will confiscate the masks and detain your children under suspicion of being little Mexican tag-team terrorists.

You'll need to make a list of everyone to shop for. If you're a woman, you'll no doubt want to buy something for:

- The neighbor watching your home
- The gay friend watching your pets
- Your best friend
- All your girlfriends at work
- The lady who lives across the hall or across the street
- The lady who does your nails
- Your mother
- Your grandmother
- Your favorite aunt

If you're a guy, you'll want to buy a one-gallon bottle of Jack Daniels for your mom so you'll have a reason to visit her more often.

What to Buy?

Who cares? Just find something cheap that will fit in your suitcase and LET'S GO!

Getting All That Crap Home

Remember that, when buying luxury items such as jewelry or watches, you'll be responsible for paying the duty after your duty-free allowance has been met. As a U.S. citizen, you're allowed around $800 in merchandise (around $1,600 in the U.S. Virgin Islands), one liter of alcohol, one carton of cigarettes and 100 cigars. But if you simply say, "I'm an American, so I can do what I want!" Customs will waive the duty. They'll also let you hang out in your very own VIP lounge, complete with a cot and a shiny metal toilet.

Chapter 24: Packing for Home

Doing Laundry

Depending on how much clothing you and your family brought on board with you, you might want to do some laundry before you pack up so that you won't have to do it when you get home. Most ships have a guest laundry room with three or more washers and dryers to be shared among 3,000 or more guests. If you're lucky, you'll be cruising with a bunch of slobs, so you'll be able to jump in there whenever you want. But if you don't feel like spending $10 for a load of laundry, you can always ask your cabin steward to get it done for you. Every cabin should have a laundry bag big that is barely big enough for one pair of socks. Just put your dirty socks in there and then pile your other dirty laundry on top of the bag and fill out the laundry slip. Your steward will then send your stuff down to the ship's laundry to be washed and pressed. Prices are usually quite reasonable. For example, here's a price list from my most recent cruise:

1. Pair of socks (white, tube): $6 ($4 more than the socks cost)
2. Pair of socks (black, dress/sandals if over 60): $7
3. Pair of blue jeans: $15 (normal), $20 (trailer-park-queen size)
4. Pair of underwear: $1,000 (after how much you've eaten this cruise, they're not touching your dirty shorts for less than a grand)

Fitting Everything Back into Your Suitcase

When they say that cruises can be magical, one of the things they're talking about is how the clothes you packed into your suitcase when you left for the cruise somehow mysteriously become too big to fit back into the suitcase when it's time to leave. If you bought a lot of souvenirs, you might want to throw some old clothes out to make room. You may also want to check your suitcase for things that don't belong to you such as those towels, that bathrobe, or your cabin steward. (A trick many stewards use is to hide in your cabin while you're packing and then jump into your suitcase when you're not looking. They've all heard that America welcomes illegal immigrants with open arms and that Donald Trump is personally waiting for them with high-paying jobs at his hotels.)

Helping Your Kids Pack

Helping your kids pack is relatively easy. Just tell them you want to play a game called Stop Your Crying Right Now and Just Throw Your Damn Clothes into the Your Stupid Suitcases as Fast as You Can and the winner wins free ice cream and pizza on Lido Deck. When your kids are leaning over their suitcases, push them in, lock them up and then place them lovingly into the hallway. After Housekeeping carts the suitcases off to the luggage hold for offloading the next morning, you'll be able to have a peaceful last night of your cruise.

Don't Pack *Everything*

It's a really good idea to attend the cruise director's debarkation talk. And, because it's a good idea, you probably won't go. Don't worry; neither will your fellow cruisers. Veteran cruisers know it's much more fun to complain about how disorganized the debarkation process is than to actually be informed and disembark smoothly. So since you're going to skip the talk, take it from me: If you're going to have your cabin steward take your luggage at night, make sure you leave some clothes out for the following day. You don't want to show up on the gangway the next morning all stinky and wrinkled, because then you might get mistaken for a hung-over crew member.

Putting Your Luggage out in the Hallway

If you decide to disembark under "self-assist" status, you'll keep your luggage in your cabin and disembark with every piece in the morning, carrying it all yourself. If you only have a carry-on bag,

116

a duffle bag or a small suitcase on rollers, this is your best bet. But if you're weighted down with steamer trunks like "Lovey and Thurston Howell" from "Gilligan's Island," then do yourself a favor and pack up early and put all your stuff in the hallway the night before debarkation so it can be offloaded for you in the morning. And make sure you keep your luggage unlocked because that's how crew members get their new clothes to take home with them after their contracts are up. Show me a Filipino at the airport in a new suit and I'll show you a first-time cruiser who forgot to lock up his suitcase.

Chapter 25: Disembarking

Debarkation Tips

If you miss the cruise director's debarkation—or "debark"—talk, don't worry. A debarkation information sheet will be sent to your cabin on the last night of your cruise. Throw it away. Then turn on your TV and find the channel with your cruise director's debarkation talk playing in a loop all day long. Pull the plug. In order to fully enjoy the debarkation process, you're going to want to just take the elevator (about a two-hour wait) down to the lobby and see what happens. There, the first thing you'll want to do is to find the cruise director. After taping a live debark talk and making sure the debark information sheet was distributed to every single cabin on the ship, he'll probably be overjoyed to answer your questions.

So, since you're not going to pay attention to anything the cruise director says all cruise long, here are my tips for a smooth and easy debarkation process:

- Be sure to wait next to the gangway, and then, every time a staff member on gangway duty asks what your "zone number" is, just say, "Nobody told me nothin' about no stupid zone number!"
- When asked to wait in one of the designated waiting areas, say "Why didn't you tell me sooner? I've been waiting here all morning. (That's especially fun to say if the staff member clearly saw you walk up a mere three seconds ago.)
- Ask a Guest Services associate what time the dining room stops serving breakfast and then show up 10 minutes after that time. Then, when the waiter tells you that the dining room is closed, throw a temper tantrum and scream, "How come nobody told me?!"

Customs & Immigration

<u>Customs & Immigration: What You'll Hear and What It'll Mean</u>

- "Please have your signed customs declaration form out and ready."
  - o "Please have your unsigned declaration form crumpled up in your suitcase so you can spend 15 minutes looking for it while everyone in line behind you starts shooting daggers at you with their eyes as the Customs agents draw their guns."
- "No cellphones."
  - o "...Except for you. *You're* an exception because *you're* special. So totally ignore the signs, even though you're on federal property and they have the right to arrest you. Unlike the other 500 people in line with you, you just got back from a long trip and you have to check on your cats."

Chapter 26: Getting Home

On the Pier

Hard to believe your cruise is over, isn't it? Oh well, time to pick up your luggage and head home. All you have to do is look for the luggage carousel displaying your zone number. What's that? Nobody told you "nothin' about no stupid zone number!"?

Ground Transportation

If you live close enough to the port to drive, then you'll be one of the first people out of the terminal. Previous jokes aside, parking is usually around $100 per week. Reasonable, if you can split it among three or four of your children.

There will also be taxis available, as well as porters to help you load your stuff into a cab. Don't forget to tip yours. If you're out of cash, just give him one of the crappy souvenirs you bought for your friends back home.

If you have a flight to catch, a shuttle bus is usually cheaper than a taxi. And the great thing about going to the airport with a busload of fellow cruisers is you get to hear the same people who did nothing but complain on the ship for seven days straight gush about how much fun they had.

Home, Sweet Home

Now that you're home, it's time to:

- Make a list of the mistakes you made on your first cruise so you can repeat them on the next one.
- Go online and inventory all the unauthorized charges to your credit card. Then call your bank and get put on hold until it's time to leave for your next cruise.
- Spend the next three months trying to nail down a time to see your friends and relatives so you can give them the

damn souvenirs you spent so much time and money trying to find instead of enjoying your limited time in your beautiful ports of call.

- Sort through all 2,000 of your photos and then spend the next year posting *every single one of them*—especially the out-of-focus ones—to your Facebook page.

There you go. Everything you wanted to know about cruising but were afraid to ask because of the answers you might get from an asshole like me.

So *bon voyage* and have fun, dude!

The End

(Of this book; hopefully, not your interest in cruising.)

About the Author

Jeff "the Fun Dude" Shaw is a stand-up comic. His writing is marked both by idealism and humanity. His stimulating satire is often infused with a singular poetic beauty. More important, he looks like Rod Stewart.

Since 1987, JTFD has performed nearly 9,000 shows across North America and the Caribbean. Jeff helped launch the "Punchliner Comedy Club" chain for Carnival Cruise Lines and was their senior comedy club manager from 2007 to 2009.

In the 1990's, Jeff wrote popular comedic essays and feature stories for Cleveland's *Scene Magazine,* Buffalo's *Art Voice,* and the online comedy publication *SHECKY! Magazine.* Jeff is also a former staff writer for Cleveland's American Greetings Corporation, responsible for hundreds of funny greeting cards and novelty items for the company's Alternative Cards Department.

You can follow Jeff on Facebook, Twitter, Google +, Instagram, and at www.jeffthefundude.com.

You can read his defunct yet proudly archived blog, "The Fun Dude Abides," at www.jeffthefundude.wordpress.com.

If you have any comments, complaints or banana nut bread recipes, you can reach Jeff at thefundude@gmail.com .

# # #

Made in the USA
Lexington, KY
22 November 2019

57248670R00068